Lord's Supper
Meditations for Disciples
on the Eucharist or Communion

for Personal Devotional Use, Small Groups or Sunday School Classes,
and Sermon Preparation for Pastors and Teachers

JesusWalk® Bible Study Series
by Dr. Ralph F. Wilson
Director, Joyful Heart Renewal Ministries

Additional books, and reprint licenses are available at:
www.jesuswalk.com/books/lord-supper.htm

Free Participant Guide handout sheets are available at:
www.jesuswalk.com/lord-supper/lords-supper-lesson-handouts.pdf

JesusWalk® Publications
Loomis, California

Paperback
ISBN-13: 978-0-9832310-7-3
ISBN-10: 0983231079

Library of Congress Control Number: 2011915108

Library of Congress subject headings:
Lord's Supper.
Lord's Supper – Biblical teaching.

Suggested Classifications
Dewey Decimal System: 265
Library of Congress: BV825

Published by JesusWalk® Publications, P.O. Box 565, Loomis, CA 95650-0565, USA.

JesusWalk is a registered trademark and Joyful Heart is a trademark of Joyful Heart Renewal Ministries.

Unless otherwise noted, all the Bible verses quoted are from the New International Version (International Bible Society, 1973, 1978), used by permission.

110823

Preface

German reformer Martin Luther (1483-1546) portrait by Lucas Cranach the Elder (1529), oil on wood, 37 x 27 cm, Uffizi Gallery, Florence.

Trying to discuss sacraments such as the Lord's Supper is dangerous, especially in a study that seeks to be non-sectarian. Many of us come from traditions with rather strict rules, such how to administer communion properly, who can be admitted to the Table, who can administer the sacrament, and what it means. I'm sad to say that in history Christians spilled each others' blood over what they believed about the Lord's Supper.

When the Swiss and German reformers met at Marburg in 1529 to find areas of agreement, Luther was so upset at Zwingli over the corporeal (that is, bodily) presence of Christ in the sacrament that he refused to shake his hand at the conclusion. I hope we can learn from the bad examples of our forebears.

I sincerely disagree at some interpretations of my Catholic brothers and sisters and they at mine, for example. But I hope we can still hold Christian fellowship around Jesus Christ as Lord, respect each other's earnestly held differences, and cherish mutual love for one another in Christ.

Unlike most studies where a whole passage is considered together, for this series of meditations we'll be pondering specific words and ideas in each chapter. There'll be a tendency to be impatient, to try to put it all together in one sitting. Struggle to resist that temptation for the sake of the process. Our goal here is to ponder, to meditate, to think deeply about, to pray over, and to internalize the various aspects of what the Lord's Supper means. We're in no hurry. Our goal is to grab hold of the Lord's Supper with such depth that this study will help enrich our practice of taking communion for years to come.

You may even find this study a bit simple, some will think simplistic. Though we're talking about mysteries here than none of us can fully plumb, I see simplicity as both a virtue and an aid to meditation. As you ponder the simple truths of the Lord's Supper and let them sink down into your spirit, you'll find yourself much richer for it when it comes time to partake of communion once more.

May God enrich your spirit as you meditate on the Lord's Supper and all that it represents.

Dr. Ralph F. Wilson
Loomis, California
July 2, 2006

Table of Contents

Reprint Guidelines

Copying the Handouts. In some cases, small groups or Sunday school classes would like to use these notes to study this material. That's great. An appendix provides copies of handouts designed for classes and small groups. There is no charge whatsoever to print out as many copies of the handouts as you need for participants.

All charts and notes are copyrighted and must bear the line:

"Copyright © 2011, Ralph F. Wilson. All rights reserved. Reprinted by permission."

You may not resell these notes to other groups or individuals outside your congregation. You may, however, charge people in your group enough to cover your copying costs. Free Participant Guide handout sheets are available at:

www.jesuswalk.com/lord-supper/lords-supper-lesson-handouts.pdf

Copying the book (or the majority of it) in your congregation or group, you are requested to purchase a reprint license for each book. A Reprint License, $2.50 for each copy, is available for purchase at

www.jesuswalk.com/books/lord-supper.htm

Or you may send a check to:

Dr. Ralph F. Wilson
JesusWalk Publications
PO Box 565
Loomis, CA 95650, USA

The Scripture says,

"The laborer is worthy of his hire" (Luke 10:7) and "Anyone who receives instruction in the word must share all good things with his instructor" (Galatians 6:6).

However, if you are from a third world country or an area where it is difficult to transmit money, please make a small contribution instead to help the poor in your community.

References and Abbreviations

BDAG   *A Greek-English Lexicon of the New Testament and Other Early Christian Literature* by Walter Bauer and Frederick William Danker, (Third Edition; based on previous English editions by W.F. Arndt, F.W. Gingrich, and F.W. Danker; University of Chicago Press, 1957, 1979, 2000)

Brown, *John*   Raymond E. Brown, *The Gospel According to John* (Anchor Bible, 2 volumes; 1966, 1970)

Bruce, *1&2 Cor* F. F. Bruce, *I & II Corinthians* (The New Century Bible Commentary; Eerdmans 1971)

DJG   Joel B. Green and Scot McKnight (editors), *Dictionary of Jesus and the Gospels* (InterVarsity Press, 1992)

DOTP   *Dictionary of the Old Testament: Pentateuch*, T. Desmond Alexander and David W. Baker (eds.) (InterVarsity Press, 2003).

Fee, *1 Cor*   Gordon D. Fee, *The First Epistle to the Corinthians* (New International Commentary on the New Testament; Eerdmans, 1987)

Hill, *Matthew*   David Hill, *The Gospel of Matthew* (The New Century Bible Commentary; Eerdmans, 1972)

ISBE   *The International Standard Bible Encyclopedia*, Geoffrey W. Bromiley (general editor), (Eerdmans, 1979-1988; fully revised from the 1915 edition).

Jeremias, *Words* Joachim Jeremias (A. Ehrhardt, tr.), *The Eucharistic Words of Jesus* (Oxford: Basil Blackwell, 1955)

Kelly	J.N.D. Kelly, *Early Christian Doctrines* (Second Edition; Harper & Row, 1958, 1960)
Life & Times	Alfred Edersheim, *The Life and Times of Jesus the Messiah* (2 volume edition; Eerdmans, 1969, reprinted from the third edition, 1886)
Marshall, *Supper*	I. Howard Marshall, *Last Supper and Lord's Supper* (Eerdmans, 1980)
Metzger, *Textual Commentary*	Bruce M. Metzger, *A Textual Commentary on the Greek New Testament* (United Bible Societies, 1971)
Morris, *1 Cor*	Leon Morris, *The First Epistle of Paul to the Corinthians* (Tyndale New Testament Commentaries; Eerdmans, 1958)
Morris, *Matthew*	Leon Morris, *The Gospel According to Matthew* (Pillar Commentary Series; Eerdmans, 1992)
NIDNTT	*New International Dictionary of New Testament Theology*, Colin Brown (editor; Zondervan, 1975-1978; translated with additions and revisions from *Theologisches Begriffslexikon zum Neuen Testament*, Coenen, Beyreuther, and Bitenhard, editors)
Strack and Billerbeck	H.L. Strack and P. Billerbeck, *Kommentar zum Neuen Testament aus Talmud und Midrasch* (München, 1956)
TDNT	*Theological Dictionary of the New Testament*, Gerhard Kittel and Gerhard Friedrich (editors), Geoffrey W. Bromiley (translator and editor), (Eerdmans, 1964-1976; translated from Theologisches Wörterbuch zum Neuen Testament, ten volume edition).

Thayer   Joseph Henry Thayer, *Greek-English Lexicon of the New Testament*
                (Associated Publishers and Authors, n.d., reprinted from 1889
                edition)

TWOT   *Theological Wordbook of the Old Testament*, R. Laird Harris, Gleason L.
                Archer, Jr., and Bruce K. Waltke, editors)

Introduction

If you're new to the Christian faith, let me provide a simple explanation of the Last Supper.

What Is the Lord's Supper?

The night before Jesus was crucified, Jesus had a last meal, called the Last Supper, with his twelve disciples. On that night Jesus compared bread to his body given as a

Pascal-Adolphe-Jean Dagnan-Bouvert (French Naturalist painter, 1852-1929), The Last Supper, oil on canvas, private collection.

sacrifice. He spoke of wine as his blood poured out for forgiveness of sins. Then he invited his disciples to partake of the bread and wine that night. Since that time Christians have partaken of the Lord's Supper, a commemoration of the Last Supper instituted by Jesus.

Different branches of the Christian Church have different practices and historical beliefs about the Lord's Supper. Roman Catholics hold a daily Mass. Many groups, including Episcopalians (Anglicans) and Lutherans, Christian Churches, partake weekly. Others, such as Baptists, Presbyterians, and Pentecostals, partake monthly. A few groups partake only once or twice a year.

When Did the Original Lord's Supper Take Place?

Scholars are not agreed whether the Last Supper took place on Passover (which seems likely according to the Synoptic Gospels – Matthew, Mark, and Luke), or the day before Passover (which can be inferred from John's Gospel). To me it makes the most sense that Last Supper took place on Passover, probably Thursday evening. Several details of the accounts seem to correspond with a Passover Seder.

What Kind of Bread Was Used?

Whether the Lord's Supper occurred on Passover or the day before, the bread they used would have been unleavened bread, since all leaven had been purged from Jewish houses for a week prior to Passover – the week-long feast of Unleavened Bread which culminated on Passover. In the Roman Catholic Church, altar breads must be made from wheat flour and water only.[1] Eastern Catholic and Orthodox churches use leavened bread made from wheat flour. Most Protestant churches don't have a rule about what kind of bread must be used for communion.

What Kind of Wine Was Used?

It wasn't until Dr. Thomas Bramwell Welch invented a way of pasteurizing and bottling grape juice in 1869 that it was possible to preserve grape juice without it fermenting. Since the grape harvest in Bible times would have taken place in September or October, wine drunk in March or April would have been fermented. Some Protestant denominations that had been part of the Temperance Movement in the early 20th century use grape juice for communion. Today it is often explained as a way not to tempt recovering alcoholics.

How Is Christ Present in Communion?

Let me lay out the main theological differences at the outset and then leave them for more fruitful meditations. The differences occur in how a person interprets Jesus' words: "This is my body." Is the "is" literal or figurative? Is Jesus teaching an exact correspondence between the bread and his body, or a metaphorical relationship between the two?

1. **Transubstantiation** (that is, "change in substance"). Roman Catholics since at least the Ninth Century AD have taught that, when consecrated by an ordained priest, the bread and wine become by a miracle the actual body and blood of Christ. The consecrated elements still they still look, feel, taste, and smell like bread and wine. but their substance is no longer bread and wine, but Christ. Since the consecrated elements are actually Christ, Catholics hold, then they should be venerated as the living Christ and that at mass a propitiatory sacrifice is offered to God. They believe in the *corporeal presence* or *Real Presence* of Christ in the sacrament, that the bread becomes Christ's body, and that when they partake they are taking in Christ's actual body. The keyword: "change."

[1] Code of Canon Law, Canon 924

2. **Sacramental Union (sometimes called Consubstantiation).** Luther taught that while the communion elements were real bread and real wine on the altar, he believed in a real corporeal presence, that somehow Christ's *corporeal presence* existed in, under, and with the communion elements – that the bread contains Christ's actual body. The keyword: "is."

3. **Symbolic and Spiritual Presence.** Following the teaching of John Calvin, most Protestants do not believe that the elements change into Christ's body or that the elements contain Christ's body. Rather, they hold that the bread and wine symbolize the body and blood of Christ and that Christ's *spiritual presence* is manifest in a special way at communion.[2] The keyword: "represents."

I'll support the third position in Chapter 1, but I'll try to do so gently, since I know that many of my Christian brothers and sisters sincerely believe differently.

Practices of the Lord's Supper

Most organized Christian churches have rather firm rules about the words and prayers to be said at communion, who can preside or administer the Lord's Supper, who can distribute it, who can receive it, preparation necessary for communicants (those who receive communion), how it should be consecrated, handled, and disposed of, and a multitude of other details. Most of these – originally, at least – were designed to protect the Lord's Supper from common and careless use. While many such practices are alive and well, I won't spend any time on them here. Different families of believers do things somewhat differently out of respect for the Holy Communion.

In this study it is not my intention to prescribe any right way or correct practice. The tradition of your own congregation can guide you in your *practice*. It's the *meaning* of the Lord's Supper that we'll look at together from the Scriptures. What we find, I believe, will unite us and help us together to appreciate the wonder of the Lord's Supper.

One more caution. As I've researched the Lord's Supper, I've become aware as never before of the centrality of the Lord's Supper in Christianity. I'm also aware that we Christians may understand and experience the Lord's Supper differently depending on our particular traditions. I call on you to join me in being humble in our study, ready to learn from Scripture and from others, ready to broaden our own experience of communion. For ultimately we are probing together what is a mystery to all of us, the

---

[2] Wayne Grudem, *Systematic Theology* (Zondervan, 1994), pp. 988-1002; M.E. Osterhaven, "Lord's Supper, Views of," in Walter A. Elwell (editor), *Evangelical Dictionary of Theology* (Baker Book House, 1984), pp. 653-656.

mystery of Christ in our midst whenever we break bread together in the Christian community.

Prayer

Father, we thank you for all our Christians brothers and sisters around the world. Though we differ in some of our worship practices, we are one in you, our God and Father and in the Lord Jesus Christ. Open our hearts to one another and to your Word, which we will be studying. And give us a deep appreciation for being included in your Table. In Jesus' name, we pray. Amen.

1. My Body, My Blood – Literal or Figurative?

Let's begin our study of the Lord's Supper with Jesus' basic statement at the Table relating bread to his body and wine to his blood. We can analyze this statement as follows:

Albrecht Dürer, "The Last Supper" (1623), woodcut.

1. **Bread** – has a relationship to – Jesus' Body

2. **Wine** – has a relationship to – Jesus' Blood

Exactly what does this mean? I wonder. Just what *is* the relationship of one to another? I realize that the Lord's Supper is a mystery that can't be reduced to pure logic. But what is Jesus saying?

The Words of Institution

Let's consider his Words of Institution of the Lord's Supper, that is, the words by which Jesus began and commanded continuance of this observance.

Matthew 26	Mark 14	Luke 22	1 Cor 11
[26]While they were eating, Jesus took bread, gave thanks and **broke it**, and gave it to his disciples, saying, "Take and eat; this is my body."	[22]While they were eating, Jesus took bread, gave thanks and **broke it**, and gave it to his disciples, saying, "Take it; this is my body."	[19]And he took bread, gave thanks and **broke it**, and gave it to them, saying, "**This is my body given for you**; do this in remembrance of me."	[23b]The Lord Jesus, on the night he was betrayed, took bread, [24]and when he had given thanks, he **broke it** and said, "**This is my body, which is for you**; do this in remembrance of me."
[27]Then he took the cup, gave thanks and offered it to them, saying, "Drink from it, all of you. [28]**This is my blood of the covenant**, which is **poured out for many for the forgiveness of sins**.	[23]Then he took the cup, gave thanks and offered it to them, and they all drank from it. [24]"This is my blood of the covenant, which is poured out for many," he said to them.	[20]In the same way, after the supper he took the cup, saying, "**This cup is the new covenant in my blood**, which is **poured out for you**."	[25]In the same way, after supper he took the cup, saying, "**This cup is the new covenant in my blood**; do this, whenever you drink it, in remembrance of me."

As you consider Jesus' words, what relationship or point of correspondence is there between the bread and his body? Between the wine and his blood?

As I suggested in the Introduction, theologians have spent lots of energy arguing about this. As I think about it, I comes down to two possibilities, using the bread in our thoughts:

1. Bread has a literal relationship to Jesus' Body
2. Bread has a figurative relationship to Jesus' Body

The Argument for a Literal Interpretation of the Words of Institution

The largest branches of the Church, the Roman Catholic and Eastern Churches, interpret Jesus' words literally, that is, they contend that the verb "is" must be taken literally, as "This is my body" rather than "This signifies my body." Catholic theologians offer several arguments for taking this literally:

1. **Jesus discourse in John 6:54-57 uses very literal language, which can only refer to the Eucharist.** Since the crowd of disciples interpreted Jesus as espousing some kind of cannibalism and stopped following him as a result, Jesus must have meant, "eat my flesh and drink my blood" literally, that is, looking forward to partaking of the Lord's Supper.[1] We'll consider this passage in detail in Chapter 9.

2. **Nowhere in the Words of Institution is a hint that a figurative interpretation should be considered.** Therefore, in the absence of any sign that this should be figurative, we must take it literally.

3. **Paul's language, "Guilty of the body and blood of the Lord" (1 Corinthians 11:27) requires that Christ is corporeally (i.e. bodily) present in the Lord's Supper.**

4. **The Church has taken the Words of Institution literally rather than figuratively from the earliest times.** This is an argument from tradition, of course, not from Scripture. But how the earliest churches understood the Lord's Supper may give us some clues to how the Apostles understood Jesus' command. (See Appendix 2, "A Brief History of Interpretation of the Real Presence.")

The Argument for a Figurative Interpretation of the Words of Institution

But there's another possibility, which has been carefully reasoned by Protestant theologians:

1. **Jesus' words should be seen in the context of many parables and figurative references.** For example, Jesus says, "I am the Vine" (John 15:1), the Door (John 10:9), the Bread (John 6:41). Jesus' main method of teaching was through parables; for Jesus, parables were not the exception but the rule, though when necessary he explained the parables to his disciples (Mark 4:34).

2. **Jesus held the bread in his hand when he said "This is my body,"** at the same time that the disciples could see his physical body. There was a clear distinction between the two. The context therefore requires a figurative interpretation.

3. **The phrase "this cup is a new covenant" (Luke 22:20) surely doesn't mean that the physical cup is the new covenant.** That phrase – is clearly symbolic and figurative. So are the words about the bread being Jesus' body.

---

[1] J. Pohle, "The Real Presence of Christ in the Eucharist," *Catholic Encyclopedia* (1908 edition). Catholic New Testament scholar Raymond E Brown, *John* 1:281-294 argues that the Eucharistic elements are clearly present in these verse.

4. **John 6:27-59 uses bold terms to explain a spiritual feeding on Christ.** This passage concludes, "The Spirit gives life; the flesh counts for nothing. The words I have spoken to you are spirit and they are life" (John 6:63), suggesting a figurative feeding rather than a literal, bodily feeding. Other indicators in the passage also point to a figurative interpretation. We'll examine this passage more fully in Chapter 9.

5. **Paul's reference to "sinning against the body and blood of the Lord" in 1 Corinthians 11:17 does not require the Real Presence to explain it.**

6. **The Real Presence in the elements (rather than a spiritual presence) isn't taught in the early church for at least 75 years and perhaps twice that.** If the Real Presence and transubstantiation were the church's primitive understanding, you'd expect much earlier a clear exposition of this doctrine. Even after an understanding of the Real Presence was common, many Church Fathers recognized a spiritual interpretation of the Words of Institution. (See Appendix 2, "A Brief History of Interpretation of the Real Presence.")

I know from personal experience the need to justify one's doctrine and practice by Scripture, even when the Scriptures don't quite fit. Looking back, I can see places where I've been guilty of that. But to me, the arguments for a figurative interpretation of the Words of Institution are quite compelling. I believe Jesus was speaking figuratively and symbolically.

Q1. How does your particular understanding of the bread and the wine (literal or figurative) help you grow closer to Christ when partaking of the Lord's Supper? (Note: This question is not your excuse to argue, but to learn from one another's personal experience of partaking.)
http://www.joyfulheart.com/forums/index.php?showtopic=457

The Body and Blood of the Lord

Having said that, we must realize that the Apostle Paul himself used the phrase, "the body and blood of the Lord" (1 Corinthians 11:27) and "body of Christ" and "blood of Christ" (1 Corinthians 10:16) with reference to the elements of the Lord's Supper. He used it figuratively, I believe. Nevertheless, his very words should keep us from a careless, flippant manner towards the elements of communion. This is a sacred meal we eat before the Lord in obedience to his words. While the elements are bread and wine, yet they are more to us, since for us they are reminders of the extent to which Jesus went for our salvation. When the minister prays a prayer of consecration, such as, "Set apart these elements from a common to a sacred use," they become sacred in the sense that we must treat them with reverence and respect, not with callous disregard as did the sinning Corinthians who Paul reprimands.

Not "Mere Symbols"

It's easy to react against some abuse or misunderstanding with an opposite but equal extreme. Some Protestants have come to refer to the elements of the Lord's Supper as "mere symbols," actually using "mere" (an adjective meaning "being nothing more than" to modify the word "symbols," as if symbols are to be despised and minimized). How sad. Millard Erickson cites one Baptist leader who calls such an extreme "the doctrine of the Real Absence" of Christ in the sacrament.[2]

As my colleague Gerald Frye has put it, "The elements are the form, but there is a power in them." The power is the healing, comforting, challenging presence and working of Jesus Christ the Lord through the Holy Spirit. To casually minimize what Jesus himself has instituted is deplorable. Rather, we must seek the One who gives power in the sacraments or ordinances, and understand as we may never before have understood what He intends to do in us through them.

Q2. How can an extreme symbolic interpretation cause a person to have too little respect for the Lord's Supper and its elements? Where is the balance, do you think?
http://www.joyfulheart.com/forums/index.php?showtopic=458

Actions on the Bread and Wine

The Real Presence controversy is based on interpreting a **verb of being** ("is"), though the original Aramaic that Jesus would have spoken wouldn't have contained such a verb.[3] The real key to understanding Jesus' intent lies instead in observing the **action verbs** contained in the Words of Institution. Most of these are pretty straightforward words – no big mystery, no deep meanings.

---

[2] Millard J. Erickson, *Christian Theology* (Second Edition; Baker Academic,1998), p. 1130.
[3] Hill, *Matthew*, p. 339. Marshall, *Last Supper*, p. 85.

"Took," Greek *lambanō*, "take hold of, grasp, take in hand."[4]

"Gave thanks" ("blessed" KJV, Matthew and Mark), *eulogeō*, means "bless." Jesus is not calling a blessing down on the bread here, but saying a prayer beginning, "Blessed art Thou, O Lord."[5]

"Gave thanks," *eucharisteō*, "to express appreciation for benefits or blessings, give thanks, express thanks, render/return thanks," especially of thanksgiving before meals.[6] In Matthew and Mark, *eulogeō* is used for the bread and *eucharisteō* for the cup, but in both Luke and 1 Corinthians *eucharisteō* is used interchangeably for the prayers of thanks during this forever special Passover meal.

"Broke," *klaō*, "break," in the New Testament only used of the breaking of bread by which the head of the household gave the signal to begin the meal.[7]

"Gave," *didōmi*, "to give, bestow, grant ... something to eat or drink."[8]

"Take," *lambanō*, see above.

"Eat," *phagō / esthiō*, "to take something in through the mouth, usually solids but also liquids, eat."[9]

"Drink," *pinō*, "to take in a liquid internally, drink."[10]

So far we've looked at the words used about the elements themselves. Most of these refer to the mechanics of Jesus praying, taking hold of the element, preparing it (by breaking), and asking the disciples to partake of it.

Words of Sacrificial Offering

But now Jesus uses terms from the vocabulary of sacrificial offerings to describe the *meaning* of these elements:

"Given" (Luke), *didōmi*, here used with the meaning, "to dedicate oneself for some purpose or cause, give up, sacrifice."[11] Used with a similar meaning at 2 Corinthians 8:5; Matthew 20:28; Mark 10:45; John 6:51; 1 Timothy 2:6; Galatians 1:4; Titus 2:14.

"For" is the preposition *hyper*, "a marker indicating that an activity or event is in some entity's interest, for, in behalf of, for the sake of someone or something.[12]

---

[4] *Lambanō*, BDAG 583-585, 1.
[5] *Eulogeō*, BDAG 407, 2.b. Morris, *Matthew*, pp. 658-659, footnote 52.
[6] *Eucharisteō*, BDAG 415-416, 2.
[7] *Klaō*, BDAG 546.
[8] *Didōmi*, BDAG 242, 2.
[9] *Phagō / esthiō*, BDAG 396, 1a.
[10] *Pinō*, BDAG 814, 1.
[11] *Didōmi*, BDAG 242, 10.
[12] *Hyper*, BDAG 1030-1031.

"Broken for" (KJV), *klaō*, appears as a variant reading in 1 Corinthians 11:24b. We'll discuss this further in Chapter 4.

"Poured out" ("shed," KJV), *ekcheō*, "cause to be emitted in quantity, pour out." In the cultic sense, "pour out" (compare Leviticus 4:7), especially of Jesus' death, "blood shed for (the benefit of) many..."[13] The preposition here also is also *hyper*, "in behalf of."

"Forgiveness" ("remission" KJV), *aphesis*, is actually a noun, but it describes an action. It means, "the act of freeing from an obligation, guilt, or punishment, pardon, cancellation."[14]

We'll study these in detail in Chapters 4 and 5, but here observe that the bread represents Jesus' body that is "given for" the disciples in a sacrificial sense. The wine represents Jesus' blood that was "poured out" or "shed" for forgiveness of sins. Both verbs clearly indicate Jesus' intention that his disciples understand his death as an intentional sacrifice.

Q3. Which action words used to describe the elements of the Lord's Supper, teach us that we are to be thinking of Jesus' sacrifice of atonement, when we partake of the Lord's Supper?
http://www.joyfulheart.com/forums/index.php?showtopic=459

Verbs of Eating and Drinking

Jesus is quite clear that the disciples are to eat the bread and all of them are to drink of the cup. What sense are we to make out of his command to eat the elements? Why? Ingesting the bread and wine, in my view:

1. **Is symbolic of nourishment and sustenance**.
2. **Connects us to Christ's sacrifice on the cross** in some mystical way that we'll explore in greater depth in Chapter 3.
3. **Is a powerful way of remembering Christ's death**, which we'll develop in Chapter 2.
4. **Is a way of renewing the Covenant,** in a way reminiscent of how covenants in the ancient Near East that were ratified by the parties, eating and drinking together. We'll develop this further in Chapter 6.

---

[13] *Ekcheō*, BDAG 312, 1a.
[14] *Aphesis*, BDAG 155, 2.

5. **Is a way to look forward to the fellowship of all the saints with Christ on the Last Day** – variously pictured as the Marriage Supper of the Lamb and eating with Abraham, Isaac, and Jacob. We'll develop this further in Chapter 10.
6. **Keeps us focused on Christ's death.** There's a tendency to turn Christianity away from a central focus on forgiveness of our sins into a society for moral improvement. The bread and wine remind us of our roots, of where we've been, of Christ's unimaginable love for us, of what Christ has done for us, and where we're headed eternally.

Q4. Which part of the meaning of the Lord's Supper is most valuable for you at this point in your spiritual journey when you partake of and meditate on the Lord's Supper?
http://www.joyfulheart.com/forums/index.php?showtopic=460

This is my body, given for you, says our Lord. This is my blood of the new covenant, shed for many for the forgiveness of sins. Take, eat. Drink deeply of it, all of you.

Prayer

Lord Jesus, how we your children have sinned against the body and blood of the Lord in the way we have become divided over what you have given to unite us. Forgive us, Lord. Forgive me. Bring peace to your body, and understanding to our inner hearts, that we might know the power that you have placed in the bread and wine, your body and your blood. In Jesus' name, we pray. Amen.

2. Remembering and Proclaiming Christ's Death (Luke 22:19b; 1 Corinthians 11:23-26)

"This is my body given for you; **do this in remembrance of me.**" (Luke 22:19b)

"23For I received from the Lord what I also passed on to you: The Lord Jesus, on the night he was betrayed, took bread, 24and when he had given thanks, he broke it and said, 'This is my body, which is for you; do this **in remembrance of me.**' 25In the same way, after supper he took the cup, saying, 'This cup is the new covenant in my blood; do this, whenever you drink it, **in remembrance of me.**' 26For whenever you eat this bread and drink this cup, you **proclaim the Lord's death** until he comes." (1 Corinthians 11:23-26)

"Symbols of the Holy Eucharist" stained glass window, St. Patrick's Roman Catholic Church, Smithtown, NY

In Chapter 1 we considered Jesus' interpretation of the bread as his body and the wine as his blood. In this chapter we consider his command to continue this observance into the future. The first two synoptic Gospels, Matthew and Mark, relate the historical event of the Lord's Supper: This is my body, this is my blood. But the account in Luke, carefully recorded from eyewitness testimony, relates an additional element of the Last Supper that night – a command to repeat this act perpetually, "until he comes."

The Command to "Do This" Continually (Luke 22:19b)

Let's look at this command carefully:

"This is my body given for you; **do this** in remembrance of me." (Luke 22:19b)

Jesus' commands in Mark and Matthew, "take, eat, etc." and in Luke "take, divide among yourselves" (22:17) are Aorist Imperative verbs in Greek. But the command, "do this," is a Present Imperative. Let me explain the difference:

- Aorist is a Greek tense which emphasizes the occurrence of an action, with no regard to its progress or duration. Often it expresses a singular, punctiliar point in time.[1] Aorist Imperative: **"Do this."**
- Present tense can carry the idea of continuous action in the present. The present imperative has a "durative force."[2] Present Imperative: **"Do this and keep on doing it."**

By the present imperative in both Luke and 1 Corinthians, we understand that Jesus intends that his disciples should *continue* to "do this."

Do what? This verb *poieō* is more than thinking. It denotes an action, "to undertake or do something that brings about an event, state, or condition, do, cause, bring about, accomplish, prepare, etc."[3] The context in Luke would be breaking and distributing bread that had a relationship to Christ's body. The context in 1 Corinthians would mean eating bread and drinking wine in a way that is related to Christ's body and blood, that is Jesus' death. In other words, Jesus' command to "do this" means that we disciples are to continue this action. The Scripture indicates that it was the early church's practice to celebrate the Lord's Supper "on the first day of the week" (Acts 20:7).

The *Last* Supper is the single, unrepeatable historical event that took place the night before Jesus' crucifixion. The *Lord's* Supper is that ordinance which is celebrated again and again when Christians gather in memory of Jesus' death.

Q1. When repeated often, doesn't the Lord's Supper run the risk of becoming mundane and lose its meaning? Why did Jesus command its repetition?
http://www.joyfulheart.com/forums/index.php?showtopic=461

Passover as a Memorial Feast

Of course, the Lord's Supper was born in the midst of a Passover feast or Seder. And Passover itself is designed as a feast of remembrance. The Lord instructed Moses:

[1] H.E. Dana and Julius R. Mantey, *A Manual Grammar of the Greek New Testament* (Macmillan, 1927), §179. F. Blass, A. Debrunner, and Robert W. Funk, *A Greek Grammar of the New Testament and Other Early Christian Literature* (University of Chicago Press, 1961), §318.
[2] Blass, Debrunner, and Funk, *Grammar*, §336.
[3] "Do," *poieō*, BDAG 839-842, 2.

"This is a day you are to commemorate; for the generations to come you shall celebrate it as a festival to the LORD – a lasting ordinance. For seven days you are to eat bread made without yeast.... Obey these instructions as a lasting ordinance for you and your descendants. When you enter the land that the LORD will give you as he promised, observe this ceremony. And when your children ask you, 'What does this ceremony mean to you?' then tell them, 'It is the Passover sacrifice to the LORD, who passed over the houses of the Israelites in Egypt and spared our homes when he struck down the Egyptians.'" (Exodus 12:14-15, 24-27)

At Passover there are a number of points of remembrance. In a contemporary Seder the table is set with:

- **Unleavened bread or Matzos** reminds them that there wasn't time for bread to rise; they left Egypt in a hurry.
- **Haroseth** represents the mortar used to build buildings for Pharaoh.
- **Bitter herbs** are reminiscent of the bitter affliction of slavery.
- **Parsley dipped in salt water** reminds them of the tears of the Jewish slaves.
- **Roasted egg** is a symbol of Spring.
- **Lamb's meat** was part of the meal (before sacrifices were ended in 70 AD). These days a shank bone reminds participants of the Passover lamb.
- **Four cups of wine**, each with a different meaning are part of the meal – representing freedom, deliverance, redemption, and release.
- **A fifth cup of wine** in the contemporary Jewish Seder, the Cup of Elijah, looks forward to the coming of the Messiah.

During the meal the youngest member of the family is coached to ask and answer questions, such as, "Why is this day different from all other days?" This prompts a retelling of the story of how God delivered the people of Israel from Egypt during the Exodus.

So the idea of a memorial meal was readily understood by Jesus' disciples.

Q2. What was the purpose of the Passover meal for future generations? Why was it to be repeated? What was to be remembered? What would have happened if the Jews had stopped remembering the Exodus?

http://www.joyfulheart.com/forums/index.php?showtopic=462

In Remembrance of Me

In both Luke and 1 Corinthians, Jesus adds a prepositional phrase that explains how and why the disciples are to undertake this action – "in remembrance of me." Though it might seem pedantic, let me look at each of these words one by one.

"In" is the common Greek preposition *eis*. In some contexts it might be translated "in, into, unto." But the word carries the idea of motion into a thing or towards a goal. Here it is used to denote a purpose, "in order to," or for the purpose of remembrance.[4]

"Remembrance," *anamnēsis*, means "remembrance, reminder, recollection." This isn't just a passive memory, but an active "reliving of vanished impressions by a definite act of will."[5]

"Of me" is the personal pronoun that modifies the word "remembrance."

The phrase could be rendered "for the purpose of remembering me" or "for the purpose of my remembrance." Either way, the meaning is pretty much the same. Jesus clearly commanded his disciples that they should continue to celebrate the Lord's Supper in order to remember him.

What should they be remembering about Jesus? His atoning death for them, of course, since in Chapter 1 we determined that this is the primary meaning of "body given for you" and "blood poured out for the forgiveness of sins."

Jesus' words, "Keep on doing this (present imperative) in my memory," or "in remembrance of me," is a purpose statement, a command that we are continually to remember his atoning death for our sins.

Q3. Why is our remembrance of Christ's death so important? What happens to Christianity if we neglect remembering in this way? What happens to us personally when we forget Christ's death?
http://www.joyfulheart.com/forums/index.php?showtopic=463

The Words of Institution in 1 Corinthians 11:23-25

Let's consider Paul's recitation of the Words of Institution:

"[23]For I received from the Lord what I also passed on to you: The Lord Jesus, on the night he was betrayed, took bread, [24]and when he had given thanks, he broke it and said, 'This is my body, which is for you; do this **in remembrance of me.**' [25]In the same

[4] *Eis*, BDAG 288-291, 4f.

[5] Johannes Behm, *anamnēsis, upomnēsis*, TDNT 1:348-349. BDAG 68.

way, after supper he took the cup, saying, "This cup is the new covenant in my blood; do this, whenever you drink it, **in remembrance of me.'** [26]For whenever you eat this bread and drink this cup, you **proclaim the Lord's death** until he comes." (1 Corinthians 11:23-26)

The words "received" (*paralambanō*[6]) and "passed on" (*paradidōmi*,[7] NIV), "handed on" (NRSV), or "delivered" (KJV) are not just ordinary conversation but technical terms describing the accurate conveying of the exact words of Jesus.[8] Just as Paul received the Words of Institution (either directly from Jesus by revelation [Galatians 1:12] or by reliable tradition), so he passed them on accurately to the Corinthian believers and to the other churches he planted.

Notice that Paul passes on a rather structured and parallel form of the Words of Institution, repeating "in remembrance of me" twice.

Proclaiming the Lord's Death (1 Corinthians 11:26)

Verse 26, however, is not part of the Words of Institution, but a comment upon them. Let's look at this sentence in detail:

"For whenever you eat this bread and drink this cup, you proclaim the
Lord's death until he comes." (1 Corinthians 11:26)

"For" (*gar*) is a conjunction, "a marker of cause or reason, for" or "marker of clarification."[9] It explains the reason or purpose for the remembrance, that is, to proclaim Christ's death.

"Whenever" (NIV) or **"as often as"** (KJV, NRSV) translate a pair of words, *hosakis*, "as often as," with *ean*, "as."[10] Every time you partake of the Lord's Supper is an occasion at which a statement is made, a proclamation is heard, that Jesus Christ gave his life as a sacrifice for the forgiveness of your sins! What a message!

"Proclaim" (NIV, NRSV) or **"shew"** (KJV) is *katangellō*, "to make known in public, with implication of broad dissemination." The word is frequently used in literature of public decrees.[11] The word is often used in the Acts and Paul for preaching the message of Jesus, for declaring the Christian gospel. Paul told the Corinthian church:

---

[6] *Paralambanō*, "to gain control of or receive jurisdiction, take over, receive" (BDAG 767-768, 2bγ).
[7] *Paradidōmi*, "to pass on to another what one knows, of oral or written tradition, hand down, pass on, transmit, relate, teach." (BDAG 761-763, 3).
[8] Fee, *1 Corinthians*, p. 548.
[9] *Gar*, BDAG 189-190, 1.
[10] *Hosakis*, BDAG 728. This is also used in Revelation 11:6.
[11] *Katangellō*, BDAG 515.

"When I came to you, brothers, I did not come with eloquence or superior wisdom as I proclaimed to you the testimony about God. For I resolved to know nothing while I was with you except **Jesus Christ and him crucified.**" (1 Corinthians 2:1-2)

The message of the cross is not only a reassuring word for believers, but also for unbelievers. The Lord's Supper is an enacted sermon about Jesus' sacrifice for sins.

Q4. (1 Corinthians 11:26) In what way is the Lord's Supper a proclamation? To whom is the proclamation made? Why is this important? What happens to the church when its proclamation shifts to a different central theme?
http://www.joyfulheart.com/forums/index.php?showtopic=464

I think it is ironic that some churches relegate the Lord's Supper to an only occasional observance, when the sacrament contains the church's central message.

The Lord's Supper is intended to be both a memorial feast and an enacted proclamation of Jesus' death for our sins. In your remembering you also proclaim the gospel of the crucified Christ to all mankind.

Prayer

Father, help us to remember Jesus' death for our sins rightly in the Lord's Supper. Help us to proclaim boldly in this sacrament Jesus' atoning death for the sins of all mankind. In Jesus' name, we pray. Amen.

3. Being Sharers in the Sacrifice (1 Corinthians 10:16, 18)

[14]Therefore, my dear friends, flee from idolatry. [15]I speak to sensible people; judge for yourselves what I say. [16]Is not the cup of thanksgiving for which we give thanks a participation in the blood of Christ? And is not the bread that we break a participation in the body of Christ? [17]Because there is one loaf, we, who are many, are one body, for we all partake of the one loaf.

[18]Consider the people of Israel: Do not those who eat the sacrifices participate in the altar? [19]Do I mean then that a sacrifice offered to an idol is anything, or that an idol is anything? [20]No, but the

Jaume Serra, "The Last Supper" (1370-1400), Tempera on wood, Museo Nazionale, Palermo.

sacrifices of pagans are offered to demons, not to God, and I do not want you to be participants with demons. [21]You cannot drink the cup of the Lord and the cup of demons too; you cannot have a part in both the Lord's table and the table of demons. [22]Are we trying to arouse the Lord's jealousy? Are we stronger than he? (1 Corinthians 10:16-22)

Those who dismiss the elements of the Lord's Supper as "mere symbols" haven't reckoned with this important passage in Paul's Letter to the Corinthians. Church members were tempted to participate in sacrifices to various Greek and Roman gods. Paul argues that take part in such a sacrifice is to become sharers – closely identified – with those sacrificed to, in this case demons that are the spiritual reality behind these false gods.

Q1. Why was Paul exhorting the Corinthians about the cup of the Lord and the cup of demons? What was going on in the church? What was the danger to the believers?

http://www.joyfulheart.com/forums/index.php?showtopic=465

As we study Paul's argument, we see a startling truth about the Lord's Supper.

— of christians

Participation, Communion, *Koinōnia* (1 Corinthians 10:16) — Read

> "Is not the cup of thanksgiving for which we give thanks a **participation** in the blood of Christ? And is not the bread that we break a **participation** in the body of Christ?" (1 Corinthians 10:16)

One word stands out because it is repeated again and again – the Greek word *koinōnia*, "participation" (NIV) also translated as "communion" (KJV) or "sharing" (NRSV). It means sharing something in common with others. The root *koinē* means common in contrast to private or sacred – common ground, common pastureland, communal property, a couple's community property. When it refers to people it means "participants, fellows." The idea is that which is shared in common with others.[1]

Paul uses this word *koinōnia* to describe the believer's relationship to the blood of Christ and to the body of Christ – that is, the sacrifice of Christ for us. We are sharers in the sacrifice of Christ for us; how can we also share in pagan sacrifices? That is Paul's argument here.

But it is worthy of meditation to consider yourself as having a share in, or perhaps a claim upon, the blood of Christ shed for you and for all your Christian brothers and sisters. You are a shareholder in the cross. In a sense, you are a participant and sharer in this sacrifice made for you. Dwell on that and it will touch you to the center of your soul.

Q2. What does *koinōnia* mean? What does it mean to "participate" or "share" in the blood of Christ?

http://www.joyfulheart.com/forums/index.php?showtopic=466

---

[1] Friedrich Hauck, "koinonos, ktl.," TDNT 3:789-809. BDAG 553 sees verse 16 as meaning: "Do not the cup and the bread mean the common partaking of the body and blood of Christ? After all, we partake of one and the same bread."

Eating a Portion of the Sacrifice for Sin

Now Paul gives an illustration of his point from the sacrificial practice of the Old Testament priesthood.

> "Consider the people of Israel: Do not those who eat the sacrifices **participate** *(koinōnos)* in the altar[2]?" (1 Corinthians 10:18)

The noun *koinōnos* is used in verse 18 to mean, "one who takes part in something with someone, companion, partner, sharer."[3] Paul is referring here to the practice of the priesthood to eat a portion of the sacrifices brought to the tabernacle or temple. A portion was eaten by the priests and a portion was burned on the altar.[4] In the case of a fellowship offering, a portion was also eaten by the offerer and his family.

The meat from sacrifices, along with the tithe, provided food for the priests and their families (Leviticus 10:12-15). But the priests' eating of the sacrifice was more than for food, as we see from the incident when Aaron's sons Nadab and Abihu were slain by God for making unrighteous offerings. Aaron and his remaining sons Eleazar and Ithamar were in deep mourning and neglected to eat the sin offering, as was required by the Law (Leviticus 6:26). When Moses found out he was angry:

> "Why didn't you eat the sin offering in the sanctuary area? It is most holy; it was given to you to take away the guilt of the community by making atonement for them before the LORD." (Leviticus 10:17)

In other words, not only the offering of the goat by fire, but also the eating of a portion by the priests, was part of the atonement process.

Sharers in the Altar (1 Corinthians 10:18)

Now that we've studied the role of the priests in the sacrifice, we can see the point Paul is making. Look again at Paul's statement:

> "Consider the people of Israel: Do not those who eat the sacrifices **participate** *(koinōnos)* in the altar?" (1 Corinthians 10:18)

---

[2] *Thusiastērion*, "altar" is "a structure on which observances are carried out, including especially sacrifices, altar," specifically here the altar of burnt offering in the courtyard of the temple or tabernacle (BDAG 463).

[3] *Koinōnos*, BDAG 553-554.

[4] Fee, *1 Corinthians*, p. 470, disagrees. He sees the reference to people sharing in the sacrificial meal in Deuteronomy 14:22-27, not the priest's share. I see the emphasis on the altar requiring this to be the priests' meal. Fee says, "Paul can only mean by 'sharers in the altar' that the participants shared together in the food on the altar."

Just as the priests were sharers in the sacrifice made on the altar of burnt offering,[3] Paul is saying that you and I, as we eat of the Lord's Supper, become sharers in the offering of Christ on the cross for our sins.

This is a very profound thought indeed! If this is too mystical for your logical, rational brain, give it time. Meditate upon this passage and its reference to Old Testament sacrifice.

Q3. In what way did the priests participate in the altar by eating of the Old Testament sacrifices? How does Paul connect this observation with our participation with Christ's sacrifice?

http://www.joyfulheart.com/forums/index.php?showtopic=467

Sharers in the Cross

There is a sense that as we partake of the Lord's Supper we become participants in the Christian altar of sacrifice – the cross. When we partake, we connect with the sacrifice and become sharers in it – in Him – in Christ's sacrifice for us.

During the Reformation, people argued about whether or not the Real Presence was in the sacrament. Whether or not that is the case, there is a Real Connection to Christ and his sacrifice in the Lord's Supper.

Yes, the Lord's Table is a memorial meal that looks back to Christ's sacrifice. But it is more. It is a meal that connects us now to Christ's sacrifice. We become participants, sharers, in a sense.

Communion

This is one reason that the Lord's Supper is called "communion" in the KJV. This word describes the real but mystical connection that the Lord's Supper provides between us and Christ. In eating and drinking we can "commune" with him and he with us.

When I partake I become afresh a sharer in Christ's sacrifice. I indicate my stake, my share, in the sacrifice by eating of the symbolic portion in the Lord's Supper.

This is not just an outward form, but a symbol with great power in it connecting you and me directly to Christ's sacrifice for our sins.

Q4. What are the implications for you personally, when you realize that in the Lord's Supper you are becoming a sharer in the sacrifice of the cross? How does that affect you? How does it change your understanding of the Lord's Supper?

http://www.joyfulheart.com/forums/index.php?showtopic=468

Prayer

Father, teach us what it means to have communion with Christ and his sacrifice for our sins. Open to us a door to fuller communion with You and your Son through the Holy Spirit. We long to draw closer to you and feel your presence. We long to know you better. Open our understanding. In Jesus' holy name, we pray. Amen.

4. My Body Given for You (Luke 22:19b)

We considered the Lord's Supper texts in larger scope. Now let's focus in on the significance of the bread which represents Jesus' body. Two of the four Lord's Supper texts comment on how Jesus' body is sacrificed for the disciples:

Luke 22:19b

- This is my body
- **given for you**
- do this in remembrance of me.

1 Corinthians 11:24b

- This is my body
- **which is for you**
- do this in remembrance of me.

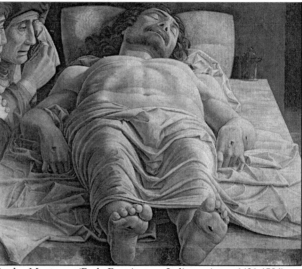

Andea Mantegna (Early Renaissance Italian painter, 1431-1506), The Lamentation over the Dead Christ, (c. 1490), Tempera on canvas, 68 x 81 cm Pinacoteca di Brera, Milan.

First, though, let's clear up a couple of textual matters. Luke 22:19b-20 is omitted in a few texts, but most ancient Greek manuscripts and modern translations retain those verses.[1]

My Body which Is Broken for You (1 Corinthians 11:24b, KJV)

A more noticeable correction in the text is the omission of the word "broken" in 1 Corinthians 24b, which was included in the KJV, but probably wasn't present in the earliest Greek manuscripts.[2] Since I grew up on an order of service based on the KJV, it's

---

[1] The KJV and most modern translations (NIV, RSV later edition, NRSV, NASB, NJB) include the longer text with the overwhelming external evidence. The "Western Text" (D it^{a,d,ff2,i,l}) omit verses 19b and 20. The longer text is included in the United Bible Societies Greek New Testament (third edition) with a {C} confidence rating (Bruce M. Metzger, *Textual Commentary*, pp. 173-177).

[2] Most modern translations include the phrase, "which is for you," omitting the word "broken." This reading is found in the Third Edition of the UBS Greek text {B}, confidence rating, and in most of the earliest texts: p^{46} Aleph* A B C* 6 33 424^c 1739* arm Origen Cyprian. The KJV includes the word "broken," with Aleph^c C^3 D^{b,c} G K P Ψ 81 614 1739^{mg} Byz Lect it^{d,g} syr^{p,h} goth, apparently derived from 'broke' in the previous clause. Other ancient texts are: "which is broken in pieces for you," in D^{gr}, and "which is given

taken me a while to get used to saying the Words of Institution without the word "broken." But I'm convinced that it's closer to Jesus' original words.[3] And the meaning hasn't changed; it still focuses on sacrifice.

John makes the point that even though the legs of those crucified on either side of Jesus were broken in order to hasten their death, Jesus was already dead so his legs were not broken:

> "These things happened so that the scripture would be fulfilled: 'Not one of his bones will be broken.'" (John 19:36, citing Psalm 34:20)

The bread in the sacrament is broken, but that is not the center of our remembrance. It is not the *breaking* of Jesus' body but the *giving* of it that we are to focus on.

Jesus' Body Given for You (Luke 22:19b)

As mentioned in Chapter 1, the key verb regarding the bread and body is "given," *didōmi*, used in Luke 22:19b with the meaning, "to dedicate oneself for some purpose or cause, give up, sacrifice."[4] The word "given" is not present but clearly implied in 1 Corinthians 11:24b, since in both accounts are followed by the preposition *hyper*, "in behalf of," which make clear that this is a reference to Jesus' voluntary sacrifice of his body for our atonement.

As we seek to meditate on Christ's body given for us, let's look at this from different angles – his body, his giving of himself, and the voluntary nature of this sacrifice.

Jesus' Body as a Sacrifice

The most common Greek noun for "body" is *sōma*, "body of a human being or animal."[5] In our text the word is used literally, but occasionally Paul uses the word figuratively of the church as his body, in the same way as we refer to a group of people as a "corporation" (from Latin *corpus*, body). Here, though, the meaning is literal.

Several New Testament passages underscore Jesus' body as a sacrifice for sin. Perhaps the most significant is from the Apostle Peter, who said,

> "He himself bore our sins in his **body** (*sōma*) on the tree, so that we might die to sins and live for righteousness; *by his wounds you have been healed*." (1 Peter 2:24).

---

for you," in vg cop[sa,bo] eth Euthalius, it[61], assimilated to Luke 22:19 "The concise expression ('which is for you') is characteristic of Paul's style," says Metzger (*Textual Commentary*, p. 562).

[3] For more information, see Appendix 4: Introduction to Textual Criticism.

[4] *Didōmi*, BDAG 242, 10.

[5] *Sōma*, BDAG 983-984, 1a.

This verse and those that precede it are filled with strong similarities of the great passage of the Suffering Servant in Isaiah 53:

> "But he was pierced for our transgressions,
> he was crushed for our iniquities;
> the punishment that brought us peace was upon him,
> and *by his wounds we are healed.*
> We all, like sheep, have gone astray,
> each of us has turned to his own way;
> and the LORD has laid on him
> the iniquity of us all." (Isaiah 53:5-6)

In his human body, Jesus bore both our sins and the punishment due us for those sins.

Q1. (1 Peter 2:24) Why do you think the Apostle Peter emphasized Jesus' physical body, when he talks about sin-bearing?

http://www.joyfulheart.com/forums/index.php?showtopic=469

> Several other passages talk about the sacrifice of Christ's body:

> "So, my brothers, you also died to the law through the **body** (*sōma*) of Christ, that you might belong to another, to him who was raised from the dead, in order that we might bear fruit to God." (Romans 7:4)

> "And by that will, we have been made holy through (*dia*) the sacrifice (*phosphora*) of the **body** (*sōma*) of Jesus Christ once for all." (Hebrews 10:10)

In a profound passage citing Psalm 40:6-8 (reflecting the Greek Septuagint translation), the writer of Hebrews sees the body of Christ as significant, prepared to be the ultimate – and willing – sacrifice.

> "Therefore, when Christ came into the world, he said:
>   'Sacrifice and offering you did not desire,
>   but a **body** (*sōma*) you prepared for me;
>   with burnt offerings and sin offerings
>   you were not pleased. '
> Then I said, 'Here I am – it is written about me in the scroll–
> I have come to do your will, O God.'" (Hebrews 10:5-7)

The body can also be referred to by the word *sarx*, usually translated "flesh" in the New Testament. However, one of its meanings is "body, physical body."[6] In the passages that follow, the NIV translate *sarx* appropriately as "body," while NRSV and KJV render it as "flesh."

> "For Christ died for sins once for all, the righteous for the unrighteous, to bring you to God. He was put to death in the **body** (*sarx*), but made alive by the Spirit." (1 Peter 3:18)

> "Therefore, since Christ suffered in his **body** (*sarx*), arm yourselves also with the same attitude, because he who has suffered in his body is done with sin." (1 Peter 4:1)

> "Therefore, brothers, since we have confidence to enter the Most Holy Place by the **blood** of Jesus, by a new and living way opened for us through the curtain, that is, his **body** (*sarx*) ...." (Hebrews 10:19-20)

One final passage demonstrates the importance to the Christian faith that Jesus' physical, bodily suffering was actual, not symbolic. An early strand of what became Docetism emphasized a strong dualism: flesh/body was inherently evil; spirit was inherently good. Therefore, the Docetists taught that Jesus only *appeared* to suffer in the flesh, but since he was a spirit being, his suffering wasn't real. The Apostle John identifies this heresy clearly:

> "This is how you can recognize the Spirit of God: Every spirit that acknowledges that Jesus Christ has come **in the flesh** (*sarx*) is from God, but every spirit that does not acknowledge Jesus is not from God. This is the spirit of the antichrist, which you have heard is coming and even now is already in the world." (1 John 4:2-3)

Q2. (1 John 4:2-3) Why does Christianity insist on a physical birth, physical suffering, and a resurrection of the physical body? How would our faith be different if Christ hadn't fully entered the human condition?

http://www.joyfulheart.com/forums/index.php?showtopic=470

Paintings of Christ's Body – Pietà and Lamentation

Roman Catholics have a long tradition of contemplating the dead body of Jesus in order to understand at a deeper level Christ's sacrifice, what he suffered for us. Paintings from this tradition are not designed to make us feel comfortable, but rather painfully aware of Christ giving his body in death as a sacrifice on our behalf.

---

[6] *Sarx*, BDAG 914-916, 2a.

The most famous of the Pietà genre is Michae-langelo's "Pietà" (1499), a massive but delicate and sensitive sculpture showing St. Mary cradling the dead body of her Son before his burial. It is an almost luminous white marble, and resides in St. Peter's Basilica in the Vatican. Ponder it as you meditate on the body of Jesus given for you.

Another "Pietà" (1471-1474) is by Giovanni Bellini, also in the Vatican. It is an amazingly detailed painting of Jesus' dead body, propped in a sitting position, surrounded by Jesus' burial party – Joseph of Arimathea, Nicodemus, and Mary Magdalene. Look at the fascinating interplay of hands that conveys a sense of deep grief.

Michelangelo (Italian painter and sculptor, 1475-1564), "Pieta" (c. 1499), marble, 5¾ x 6 feet, 174 x 195 cm, St. Peter's Basilica.

A third Pietà on which to meditate is Lucas Cranach the Elder's "The Trinity" (early 16th century). Observe the haunted pain in the Father's eyes as he holds the body of our crucified Savior. Our salvation is indeed costly to the Godhead.

A second genre centers around the deposition of the body of Christ in the tomb. Andea Mantegna's, "Lamentation over the Dead Christ" (c. 1490), shown at the beginning of this chapter, is disturbing. It views Christ's unclothed body as it lies on the tomb slab, viewed from his feet, the body skillfully foreshortened by the artist.

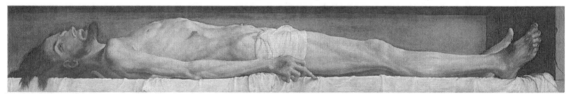

Hans Holbein the Younger, "The Body of the Dead Christ in the Tomb" (1521), Oil on wood, 30,5 x 200 cm, Kunstmuseum, Öffentliche Kunstsammlung, Basle.

Finally, I am struck by Hans Holbein the Younger's "Body of the Dead Christ in the Tomb" (1521). It is a ghastly, realistic painting of Christ's body lying on its back on the tomb slab, unclothed, with blackened hands. My God, what have you done for us?

Jesus Gave Himself to Rescue and Ransom Us

We've explored the aspect of Christ's body. Now let's look at his giving of himself.

"This is my body **given for you**." (Luke 22:19b)

There are several verses in the New Testament that use the verb *didōmi*, "give," with the preposition *hyper*, "in behalf of."

"This bread is my flesh, which I will **give for the life of the world**." (John 6:51b)

"For there is one God and one mediator between God and men, the man Christ Jesus, who **gave himself as a ransom for** all men...." (1 Timothy 2:5-6)

"... the Lord Jesus Christ, who **gave himself for our sins** to rescue us from the present evil age, according to the will of our God and Father." (Galatians 1:3-4)

"... Jesus Christ, who **gave himself for us to redeem us** from all wickedness and **to purify** for himself a people that are his very own, eager to do what is good." (Titus 2:13-14)

"The Son of Man did not come to be served, but to serve, and to **give his life as a ransom for** (*anti*[7]) **many**." (Matthew 20:28 = Mark 10:45)

"Christ loved us and **gave himself up** (*paradidōmi*) **for** (*hyper*) **us** as a fragrant offering and sacrifice to God." (Ephesians 5:2)

Paradidōmi is used here with the meaning, "hand over, turn over, give up a person," as a technical term of police and courts, "hand over into the custody of."[8] Christ "turned himself in" for us, "the Righteous for the unrighteous, that he might bring us to God" (1 Peter 3:18, RSV).

Q3. Look at the verses above which include both the word "give" and a preposition that means "in behalf of." According to these verses, what was the purpose of Jesus giving himself in sacrifice?
http://www.joyfulheart.com/forums/index.php?showtopic=471

He Voluntarily Laid Down His Life to Defend Us

This voluntary element of the Lord's Supper words is valuable for us to ponder as well.

"This is my body **given for you**." (Luke 22:19b)

The Garden of Gethsemane was an instance where the mystery of Jesus' human and divine nature is peeled back for a moment to reveal his voluntary submission. He agonizes in prayer:

[7] The preposition *anti* carries the basic meaning "instead of, in place of," here indicating a process of intervention, "in behalf of, for someone," so that *anti* becomes = *hyper* (BDAG 87-88, 3).
[8] *Paradidōmi*, BDAG 1b.

"'Father, if you are willing, take this cup from me; yet not my will, but yours be done.' An angel from heaven appeared to him and strengthened him. And being in anguish, he prayed more earnestly, and his sweat was like drops of blood falling to the ground." (Luke 22:42-44)

His holy nature recoils from bearing sin. His physical body is profused with sweat as he struggles in prayer, great drops of it falling from his body like blood.[9] Later, when the soldiers appear to arrest him, Peter begins to defend with a sword, succeeding in cutting of an ear of the high priest's servant Malchus. But after having surrendered to the Father's will in Gethsemane, Jesus is resolute. He commands Peter,

"Put your sword away! Shall I not drink the cup the Father has given me?" (John 18:11)

"Do you think I cannot call on my Father, and he will at once put at my disposal more than twelve legions of angels?" (Matthew 26:53)

Jesus wasn't arrested violently. He voluntarily allowed the soldiers to take him into custody. "This is my body **given for you**" (Luke 22:19b).

Tithēmi is a very common Greek word that means "to put or place in a particular location, lay, put."[10] It is used in a similar phrase with the preposition *hyper*, "in behalf of," that represents the voluntary nature of giving his body, "to lay down his life."

"I am the good shepherd. The good shepherd **lays down his life** for (*hyper*) the sheep." (John 10:11, 14-15, 17)

"Greater love has no one than this, that he **lay down his life** for (*hyper*) his friends." (John 15:13)

Q4. How does Jesus' voluntarily laying down his life for you encourage you? How does it speak to your value and worth as a person? What does it inspire you to do?
http://www.joyfulheart.com/forums/index.php?showtopic=472

When we remember Jesus' body given for us, it is meant to fashion and mold us as both recipients of his grace and dispensers of that grace. "Do this in remembrance of me," Jesus said.

---

[9] Some have interpreted this as sweat mixed with blood caused by broken capillaries brought on by stress, but I think the simplest interpretation is to see the relationship between sweat and blood in the drops falling.

[10] *Tithēmi*, BDAG 1003-1004.

Prayer

Father, reproduce in us your own heart, I pray. Stretch us as we remember Jesus' giving his body in sacrifice. Work in us that same spirit of unconditional love and committed sacrifice, that we might represent you well on this earth. In Jesus' name, we pray. Amen.

5. My Blood Poured Out for Many (Matthew 26:28)

[27]"Then he took the cup, gave thanks and offered it to them, saying, 'Drink from it, all of you. [28]This is **my blood** of the covenant, which is **poured out for many for the forgiveness of sins.**'" (Matthew 26:27-28)

"Then he took a cup, and after giving thanks he gave it to them, and all of them drank from it. He said to them, 'This is **my blood** of the covenant, which is **poured out for many.**'" (Mark 14:23-24)

"In the same way, after the supper he took the cup, saying, 'This cup is the new covenant in **my blood, which is poured out for you.**'" (Luke 22:20)

"In the same way, after supper he took the cup, saying, 'This cup is the new covenant in **my blood;** do this, whenever you drink it, in remembrance of me.'" (1 Corinthians 11:25)

Let's focus on the sentence:

> "This is my blood ... which is poured out for many for the forgiveness of sins.'" (Matthew 26:28)

To understand Jesus' words, we need to explore how blood was used in the Old Testament, the role of the Paschal lamb, and the roots of Jesus' phrase "poured out for many." In Chapter 6 we'll consider the covenantal aspect of the Lord's Supper, where the

Mel Gibson's "The Passion of the Christ" (2004, NewMarket Films) is one of the bloodiest depictions of Christ's scourging and crucifixion. The part of Jesus is acted by James Caviezel.

key verse is from Exodus: "Moses then took the blood, sprinkled it on the people and said, 'This is the blood of the covenant that the LORD has made with you in accordance with all these words.'" (Exodus 24:8). But in this chapter let's explore the blood of Christ shed for us.

Blood Reserved for Atonement

From the earliest times, God commanded his people – from Noah on down – not to drink blood (Genesis 9:4), even though this was a common practice of their pagan neighbors:

> "Any Israelite or any alien living among them who eats any blood – I will set my face against that person who eats blood and will cut him off from his people. For the life of a creature is in the blood, and I have given it to you to make atonement for yourselves on the altar; it is the blood that makes atonement for one's life." (Leviticus 17:10-11)

There are two views of this passage. One is that blood represents life, for "The life of the flesh is in the blood." The other is that the blood denotes death, specifically life that is offered up in death. The second is much closer to Biblical thought. Victor Hamilton writes:

> "Atonement for sins was made by the sacrifice of the life of animals as a substitution for one's own life, and the shedding of blood was the most important element in the expiation of sin. Hence, the prohibition on human imbibing. It was too sacred for ordinary man to handle."[1]

Blood Sacrifices in the Old Testament

When sin was concerned, blood sacrifices were mandatory in the Old Testament:

> "In fact, the law requires that nearly everything be cleansed with blood, and without the shedding of blood[2] there is no forgiveness." (Hebrews 9:22)

When a person sinned, the Law prescribed that a lamb or goat without defect would be brought. The offender was to lay his hand on the head of the sin offering and slaughter it before the Lord at the tabernacle or temple. Then the priest was to take the blood, sprinkle some on the horns of the altar of burnt offering and pour out the rest at the base of the altar (Leviticus 4:27-35). There was also a daily sacrifice for the sins of the people (Exodus 29:38) as well as an annual Day of Atonement (Yom Kippur, Leviticus 16).

People in our culture look at blood sacrifice with revulsion, as well we should. It is an awful thing. But this is not some primitive practice to appease a bloodthirsty God in order to ward off evil. Rather it is an act of God's mercy and grace (Psalm 51:16-17). Let me explain.

---

[1] Victor P. Hamilton, *dām*, TWOT #436.
[2] *Haimetekchusia*, "shedding of blood," is a compound noun from *haima*, "blood," + *ekchunō*, "shed, pour out" (Thayer).

Sacrifice was God's way of teaching us the seriousness of sin; it was not an end in itself. Instead of snuffing out a person for sin or rebellion, God offered a way for the forgiveness of sins, the death of an animal instead of a person. A lamb or goat or bull was costly, teaching that sin is costly. The requirement of a blood sacrifice for sin was ultimately fulfilled in Christ, who is the sacrifice for our sins, once and for all. No further sacrifice can be made. Any subsequent sacrifice of an animal is an affront to God, suggesting that the sacrifice of his Son was not enough.

When I was in college I can remember being confused about this issue. Does one have to understand and accept Jewish law before one can become a Christian? Fortunately, no! Christ has died for our sins whether or not we understand how he fulfilled the Law. Is fulfillment of the Old Testament law of sacrifice really what Jesus' crucifixion was all about? Yes, I finally concluded. If we are to understand accurately why the cross was necessary, we must turn to Old Testament sacrifice.

Jesus fulfills all of the required sacrifices for sin. The Law required an animal for a human life (the lesser for the greater), but God provided his own Son as a sacrifice for our sins (the greater for the lesser), bringing us to God.

Q1. How were Old Testament sacrifices a way of God showing grace and mercy to his people?
http://www.joyfulheart.com/forums/index.php?showtopic=473

Sacrificing the Paschal Lamb

The night Jesus instituted the Lord's Supper was Passover night. Jesus and his disciples were seated around a low table partaking of the Passover Meal, the Paschal lamb, slain earlier in the day for the members of this band of disciples. Passover looked back at least 1200 years to Israel's deliverance from Egypt. That night, God had directed that a lamb be slain for every household, to protect the firstborn of that family from being slain.

> "Then they are to take some of the blood and put it on the sides and tops of the door-frames of the houses where they eat the lambs....
>
> "On that same night I will pass through Egypt and strike down every firstborn – both men and animals – and I will bring judgment on all the gods of Egypt. I am the LORD. The blood will be a sign for you on the houses where you are; and when I see the blood,

> I will pass over you. No destructive plague will touch you when I strike Egypt." (Exodus 12:7, 12-13)

Jesus not only fulfilled the sacrificial laws, he also fulfilled Passover. Paul writes:

> "Christ, our Passover lamb, has been sacrificed." (1 Corinthians 5:7)

Poured Out

Now let's examine in greater detail the words in our passage:

> "This is my blood ... which is poured out for many for the forgiveness of sins.'" (Matthew 26:28)

The verb "poured out" ("shed," KJV), which we saw in Chapter 1, is *ekcheō*, "cause to be emitted in quantity, pour out." In the cultic sense, "pour out" (compare Leviticus 4:7), especially of Jesus' death, "blood shed for (the benefit of) many..."[3] The expression "shed blood" is used of the violent slaying of Old and New Testament martyrs (Matthew 23:35; Romans 3:15 = Isaiah 59:7; Acts 22:20; Revelation 16:6).[4] Here is a strange confluence of two ideas: (1) blood shed as part of a ritual sacrifice and (2) blood violently shed to martyr a servant of God. With this word Jesus is explaining that his death on the cross – violent and unrighteous as it might seem – is also a sacrifice of atonement for sin. The cruelty of the cross does not signal the tragic end to a promising ministry, but God's plan of redemption for all mankind.

The purpose of this violent sacrifice is made clear with two other words. In the phrase, "for many," the preposition "for" *peri*, here means, "a marker of events which are indirectly involved in a beneficial activity, 'on behalf of.'"[5] Jesus is saying that his blood is being shed for the benefit of others.

Q2. Why did Jesus refer to the violent nature of his death in the Words of Institution? What did this probably mean to the disciples at the time? What did it probably mean to them later?

http://www.joyfulheart.com/forums/index.php?showtopic=474

---

[3] *Ekcheō*, BDAG 312, 1a.
[4] Johannes Behm, *ekcheō*, TDNT 2:467-469.
[5] Louw & Nida, *New Testament Greek-English Lexicon*, §90.39. In other parallels to the Words of Institution, this is *hyper*, "in behalf of." Ernst Harald Reisenfeld (*peri*, TDNT 6:53-56) notes that during the Hellenistic period, the distinction between *peri* and *hyper* fades to some degree, with the result that *peri* with the genitive can be used in the sense, "on behalf of, for."

Poured Out for Many

Let's explore another interesting word: "many." Jesus says, "This is my blood ... which is poured out for **many** for the forgiveness of sins'" (Matthew 26:28). Jesus also uses this same phrase, "for many," in Mark 10:45 = Matthew 20:28:

> "For even the Son of Man did not come to be served, but to serve, and to give his life as a ransom **for many**."

Why? Jesus is making a clear and direct reference to the Suffering Servant passage of Isaiah 53 that he closely identified with his own ministry:

> "After the suffering of his soul,
> he will see the light [of life] and be satisfied ;
> by his knowledge my righteous servant will justify **many**,
> and he will bear their iniquities.
> Therefore I will give him a portion among the great,
> and he will divide the spoils with the strong,
> because he **poured out** his life unto death,
> and was numbered with the transgressors.
> **For he bore the sin of many**,
> and made intercession for the transgressors." (Isaiah 53:11-12)

In Isaiah 53 we see the very center of the Words of Institution – Jesus' voluntary sacrifice.

Jesus doesn't use the phrase "for many" to somehow limit his forgiveness to only some, rather than all of mankind (1 John 2:2; John 1:29). Rather he uses that phrase from Isaiah 53:13 so that the disciples will recall the entire Suffering Servant passage and from it gain understanding of the reason for his death.

Q3. Why did Jesus purposely point his disciples to the phrasing found in Isaiah 53? How does this chapter help explain the meaning of Jesus' death?
http://www.joyfulheart.com/forums/index.php?showtopic=475

Christ's Blood in the New Testament

In our day, certain branches of the Christian Church are embarrassed by the blood of Christ. Some have stricken it from hymnals as too graphic, too morbid, too primitive an interpretation of Jesus' death. But the New Testament is not shy about the subject. It is very important to notice that most often the word "blood" in the New Testament becomes a *symbol* for the whole concept of Jesus' sacrificial, atoning death, not just a mention of his blood as somehow separated from his atoning death. Now, with that in mind, here are some passages to ponder:

Redemption

"You were **redeemed** ... with the precious blood of Christ." (1 Peter 1:18-19).

"**Redemption** through his blood, the forgiveness of sins...." (Ephesians 1:7)

Entering "the Most Holy Place once for all by his own blood, having obtained **eternal redemption.**" (Hebrews 9:12)

Purchase (a concept closely related to redemption)

"... With your blood you **purchased** men for God." (Revelation 5:9)

"The church of God, which he **bought** with his own blood." (Acts 20:28)

Forgiveness and Atonement

"God presented him as a **sacrifice of atonement**, through faith in his blood." (Romans 3:25)

"Since we have now been **justified** by his blood...." (Romans 5:9)

Sanctification, Cleansing, and Purification from Sin

"How much more ... will the blood of Christ ... **cleanse our consciences.**" (Hebrews 9:14)

"... The blood of Jesus, his Son, **purifies** us from all sin." (1 John 1:7)

"... Who have been chosen ... through the **sanctifying** work of the Spirit, for obedience to Jesus Christ and sprinkling by his blood...." (1 Peter 1:2)

"Jesus also suffered outside the city gate **to make the people holy** through his own blood." (Hebrews 13:12)

Freedom and Victory over Sin and Satan

"To him who loves us and has **freed** us from our sins by his blood...." (Revelation 1:5)

"They **overcame** him by the blood of the Lamb and by the word of their testimony...." (Revelation 12:11)

Reconciliation to and Peace with God

"But now in Christ Jesus you ... have been **brought near** through the blood of Christ." (Ephesians 2:13)

"... Through him to **reconcile** to himself all things ... by making peace through his blood, shed on the cross." (Colossians 1:19-20)

"We have **confidence to enter** the Most Holy Place by the blood of Jesus." (Hebrews

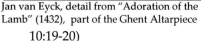

Jan van Eyck, detail from "Adoration of the Lamb" (1432), part of the Ghent Altarpiece 10:19-20)

Detail from "Adoration of the Lamb" (1497-98) woodcut by Albrecht Dürer.

"May the **God of peace**, who through the blood of the eternal covenant brought back from the dead our Lord Jesus...." (Hebrews 13:20-21)

Depictions of the Blood of Christ

In the New Testament, Jesus' blood is not especially glorified, though Peter refers to "the precious blood of Christ" (1 Peter 1:19). But by the middle ages Christ's blood had become a focus of worship. You see paintings and woodcuts of angels collecting in a chalice the blood from Christ's wounds on the cross (John 19:34), or from the slain Lamb on the throne in Revelation (Revelation 5:6). Perhaps the most graphic depiction of the blood of Christ in our own day is Mel Gibson's portrayal of the scourging of Jesus in his movie "The Passion of the Christ" (NewMarket Films, 2004), with Jesus' mother and Mary Magdalene wiping up his blood which covered the courtyard where Jesus' scourging took place.

Songs about the Blood of Jesus

The last couple of centuries has produced a number of gospel songs that focus on the blood of Christ, including:

"There Is a Fountain Filled with Blood, Drawn from Emmanuel's Veins," words by William Cowper (1772), music: 19th century American camp meeting tune.

"There Is Power in the Blood," words and music by Lewis E. Jones (1899).

"What Can Wash Away My Sin? Nothing but the Blood of Jesus," words and music by Robert Lowry (1876).

"Oh, the Blood of Jesus, It Washes White as Snow" (unknown author)

"Are You Washed in the Blood?" words and music by Elisha A. Hoffman (1878).

"The Blood Will Never Lose Its Power," by Andraé Crouch (©1966 by Manna Music, Inc.)

It is indeed valuable to ponder the blood of Christ and the suffering that Jesus endured for us. But it is possible to linger so long on the morbid *details* of his death that we forget the *meaning* of his death for us. Jesus' Words of Institution point to the *meaning* of the cup:

"This is my blood ... which is poured out for many for the forgiveness of sins.'" (Matthew 26:28)

Poured Out for the Forgiveness of Sin

The purpose of that sacrifice, of course, is forgiveness, pardon, freeing from sin.

"Forgiveness" ("remission" KJV), *aphesis*, means, "the act of freeing from an obligation, guilt, or punishment; pardon, cancellation."[6] The object of forgiveness is "sins" (*hamartia*), the generic word to describe all kinds of sin and guilt.

Jesus deliberately died so that you might be freed from the burden and guilt of your sin. Some have characterized Christianity as a fear- and guilt-driven religion. They have it wrong. God doesn't hold our sins over our heads with the threat of hell and condemnation. Instead, he forgives our sins fully, accepting Jesus' sacrifice for the forgiveness of sins as payment in full for your debt to God and for mine. What good is a such an act to compel compliance to the rules of a church? None at all, if the forgiveness is full and complete, never to be brought back upon us again (Isaiah 43:25; Jeremiah 31:34; Psalm 103:12; Micah 7:19).

What have you been carrying, my friend? What burden? What guilt? For what misdeed of the past have you been beaten down by self-reproach and guilt? Then partake of the Lord's Supper in full faith, listening carefully to the words:

"This is my blood ... which is poured out for many for the forgiveness of sins.'" (Matthew 26:28)

---

[6] *Aphesis*, BDAG 155, 2. Rudolf Bultmann, *aphiēmi*, TDNT 1:509-512.

As you drink of the cup, you are affirming that Christ's blood was shed for your forgiveness and your pardon. Instead of being a club to beat you into obedience, God lays down the club completely. The resulting motivator is no longer fear or guilt, but love.

> "There is no fear in love. But perfect love drives out fear, because fear has to do with punishment. The one who fears is not made perfect in love. We love because he first loved us." (1 John 4:19)

This is news almost too good to be true, but it is the message of grace found the Old Testament and the New. Paul the murderer wrote, "Here is a trustworthy saying that deserves full acceptance: Christ Jesus came into the world to save sinners – of whom I am the worst" (1 Timothy 1:15). What have you done that is too great for Christ to have atoned for on the cross? Nothing. No sin is too great for his mercy. No iniquity too heinous that he cannot forgive it because of the violent shedding of his blood as a sacrifice for you.

And so the invitation is open to you and to all:

> "The Spirit and the bride say, 'Come!' And let him who hears say, 'Come!' Whoever is thirsty, let him come; and whoever wishes, let him take the free gift of the water of life" (Revelation 22:17).

Q4. What do the Words of Institution say to us about forgiveness? Why is it important for us to repent of known sin before taking the Lord's Supper?
http://www.joyfulheart.com/forums/index.php?showtopic=476

Prayer

Thank you, O Lord, for your love for us, that led you to allow your blood to be shed in a violent death that we might find forgiveness, redemption, cleansing, and the peace that comes from wholeness in you. Thank you. In Jesus' holy name, we pray. Amen.

6. A New Covenant in My Blood (1 Corinthians 11:25)

All four accounts of the Words of Institution include the concept of a covenant in Jesus' blood.

> "This is my blood of the **covenant**[1]...." (Matthew 26:28)

> "This is my blood of the **covenant**[2]...." (Mark 14:24)

> "This cup is the **new covenant** in my blood...." (Luke 22:20)

> "This cup is the **new covenant** in my blood...." (1 Corinthians 11:25)

"The Last Supper," Capitol Drive Lutheran Church, Milwaukee, Wisconsin, designed by Peter Dohmen, installed 1956-67.

While the phrase "new covenant" appears to be omitted in the earliest manuscripts in Matthew and Mark, it is clearly present in Luke 22:20 and 1 Corinthians 11:25. In Chapter 5 we considered Jesus' blood being shed for forgiveness of sin. In this chapter let's examine the new covenant that Jesus establishes this night in his blood.

Covenants in the Old Testament

Let's begin by turning to the Old Testament. The very word "Testament" is translated "covenant," the Hebrew word *berît*, and the Greek noun *diathēkē*. A covenant is "a solemn commitment guaranteeing promises or obligations undertaken by one or both

[1] In Matthew 26:28 the earliest manuscripts omit the word "new" (p[37,45] Aleph B L Θ 33 cop[bo(ms)]), while many later manuscripts include it (A C D K W Δ Π *Byz Lect* vg, etc.) apparently from the influence of its presence in both Luke 22:20 and 1 Corinthians 11:25. If it were present originally in Matthew, there would be no reason to omit it. The United Bible Societies Editorial Committee gave the reading of "covenant" by itself a {B} likelihood of being the original (with {A} being the highest certainty ranking) (Metzger, *Textual Commentary*, p. 64).

[2] In Mark 14:24, the earliest manuscripts omit the word "new" (Aleph B C D* L W Θ Ψ it[d,k] cop[sa(ms), bo] geo[1]), while many later manuscripts include it (A K P X Δ Π f1 f13 it[most] vg syr[s,p,h] cop[sa] geo *Byz Lect*). The likelihood is pretty high {B} that the original lacks "new" (Metzger, p. 113).

covenanting parties."[3] Between nations a covenant is a treaty, an alliance. Between individuals it is a pledge or agreement. Between a king and his subjects it is a constitution. Between God and man it is a relationship with promises of blessing for keeping the covenant and curses for breaking it. Covenants were often ratified by signs, a solemn oath, and a meal. Sacrifice was often part of the process of ratifying a covenant, too, hence the phrase "to cut a covenant" (Genesis 15:9-10, 17; Jeremiah 34:18).[4]

We see a number of covenants in the Bible: God's covenant with Noah (Genesis 6:8; 9:9-17), Abraham and his descendents (Genesis 15:18; 17:2-21), Moses and the people of Israel at Mt. Sinai (Exodus 19:5; 24:7-8; 31:16; 34:10, 27; etc.).

Provisions of the Old Covenant

After God had delivered the Israelites from Egypt, he had them gather at the base of Mt. Sinai. There Moses went up to meet Him and received the Law, that is, the commandments associated with the Covenant that God was making with them. Though this is a complex subject, in essence God as King makes a solemn covenant with the Israelites to be their God and they to be his people. The covenant binds each party to solemn obligations:

God's Obligations

1. God will be with Israel and lead them on their journey.
2. God will protect his people.
3. God will provide for and bless his people.

Israel's Obligations

1. Exclusive love for and allegiance to God, no other gods.
2. Obedience to God's commandments.

Hardly has God given Moses the provisions of the Covenant in the Ten Commandments, when the Israelites build a golden calf, worship it, and attribute to it the salvation that God has brought. It is an amazing mark of God's great mercy that he forgives their sin and offers a second set of tablets to them. Here is the record of the ratification of this Covenant:

> "[3]When Moses went and told the people all the LORD's words and laws, they responded with one voice, 'Everything the LORD has said we will do.' [4]Moses then wrote down everything the LORD had said.

---

[3] Paul R. Williamson, "Covenant," DOTP 139-155.
[4] Elmer B. Smick, *berît*, TWOT #282a. Joachim Guhrt, "Covenant," NIDNTT 1:365-372.

He got up early the next morning and built an altar at the foot of the mountain and set up twelve stone pillars representing the twelve tribes of Israel. [5]Then he sent young Israelite men, and they offered burnt offerings and sacrificed young bulls as fellowship offerings to the LORD. [6]Moses took half of the blood and put it in bowls, and the other half he sprinkled on the altar. [7]Then he took the Book of the Covenant and read it to the people. They responded, 'We will do everything the LORD has said; we will obey.'

[8]Moses then took the blood, sprinkled it on the people and said, 'This is the **blood of the covenant** that the LORD has made with you in accordance with all these words.'

[9]Moses and Aaron, Nadab and Abihu, and the seventy elders of Israel went up [10]and saw the God of Israel. Under his feet was something like a pavement made of sapphire, clear as the sky itself. [11]But God did not raise his hand against these leaders of the Israelites; **they saw God, and they ate and drank**." (Exodus 24:3-11)

Sadly, however, the history of Israel is one of sin, disobedience, and worship of false gods, followed by God's judgment and restoration of a remnant of God's people. The Covenant is clear: man's part is to love God only and to obey him. That, man seems unable to do for very long. The Covenant fails because of man's weakness.

Q1. (Exodus 24:3-11) How was the covenant with Israel ratified? What promise did the people make twice in this passage? What was sacrificed? What was sprinkled? What was eaten?
http://www.joyfulheart.com/forums/index.php?showtopic=477

God's Promise of a New Covenant

In the midst of one of these cycles of falling away from obedience to God, God promises a New Covenant through Jeremiah the prophet:

"[31]'The time is coming,' declares the LORD,
'when I will make a **new covenant**
with the house of Israel
and with the house of Judah.
[32]It will not be like the **covenant**
I made with their forefathers
when I took them by the hand
to lead them out of Egypt,
because they **broke my covenant**,
though I was a husband to them,'
declares the LORD.

^{33}'This is the **covenant** I will make with the house of Israel
after that time,' declares the LORD.
**'I will put my law in their minds
and write it on their hearts**.
I will be their God,
and they will be my people.
^{34}No longer will a man teach his neighbor,
or a man his brother, saying, "Know the LORD,"
because **they will all know me**,
from the least of them to the greatest,'
declares the LORD.
'For **I will forgive their wickedness
and will remember their sins no more**.'" (Jeremiah 31:31-34)

This promise of the New Covenant, cited in the New Testament (Hebrews 8:6-13; 10:16-17), had echoed down the ages in the consciousness of pious Jews. So when Jesus lifted a cup, blessed God, and spoke the Words of Institution over it, the hair must have risen on the necks of all the disciples. This *was* something new! This was the Institution of the *New Covenant*!

"This cup is the **new covenant** in my blood...." (Luke 22:20)

Provisions of the New Covenant

What are the provisions of the New Covenant? On our part: Faith in God. Trust in God. Belief that Jesus was God in the flesh. On God's part it is salvation, eternal life, forgiveness of all our sins through the death of his Son. In addition is the provision of the Holy Spirit to live within us and enable us to follow Christ. Only a few special people received the Spirit in the Old Covenant – prophets, some kings, some elders. But the average person wasn't included. Under the New Covenant it's different:

"Repent and be baptized, every one of you, in the name of Jesus Christ for the forgiveness of your sins. And you will receive the gift of the Holy Spirit. The promise is for you and your children and for all who are far off – for all whom the Lord our God will call." (Acts 2:38-39)

"You, however, are controlled not by the sinful nature but by the Spirit, if the Spirit of God lives in you. And if anyone does not have the Spirit of Christ, he does not belong to Christ. But if Christ is in you, your body is dead because of sin, yet your spirit is alive because of righteousness. And if the Spirit of him who raised Jesus from the dead is living in you, he who raised Christ from the dead will also give life to your mortal bodies through his Spirit, who lives in you." (Romans 8:9-11)

"If we walk in the light, as he is in the light, we have fellowship with one another, and the blood of Jesus, his Son, purifies us from all sin.... If we confess our sins, he is faithful and just and will forgive us our sins and purify us from all unrighteousness." (1 John 1:7, 9)

The law that was external and depended upon human will and discipline to perform is now internalized in the Holy Spirit. We live in Christ, connected to Christ by the Holy Spirit, and we have fellowship with God. It is new! It is powerful! It is now!

Q2. (Jeremiah 31:31-34) How does the promised New Covenant differ from the Old Covenant? What are the promises God makes in the New Covenant? What are *our* responsibilities under the New Covenant?
http://www.joyfulheart.com/forums/index.php?showtopic=478

Confirmation of the Covenant at a Meal

At the Last Supper Jesus holds up a cup, probably the Fourth Cup of the Seder, and invests it with new meaning:

"In the same way, after supper he took the cup, saying, 'This cup is the new covenant in my blood; do this, whenever you drink it, in remembrance of me.'" (1 Corinthians 11:25)

Many ancient covenants were confirmed or sealed by a sacrifice followed by a covenant meal between the parties. For example in Exodus 24:11, quoted above, after the covenant was given, God invited the 70 elders up on the mountain and "they saw God, and they ate and drank." We probably see other instances of sacrifices followed by a covenant meal in covenants between Isaac and Abimelech (Genesis 26:30), Laban and Jacob (Genesis 31:46, 53-54); and Moses, the Israelites, and Jethro (Exodus 18:12). Eating fellowship offerings in the presence of the Lord probably has a similar idea of peace between all parties (Deuteronomy 27:7).

If the 70 elders ate in God's presence as representatives of the people of God to confirm the Old Covenant (Exodus 24:11), now the 12 apostles eat in Jesus' presence as the beginnings of the new people of God to confirm the New Covenant.

The Lord's Supper as Confirming the Covenant

It seems clear by Jesus' words at the table that the Last Supper was a kind of covenant meal, where Jesus introduces the New Covenant in his blood:

> "Then he took the cup, gave thanks and offered it to them, saying, 'Drink from it, all of you. This is my blood of the covenant, which is poured out for many for the forgiveness of sins.'" (Matthew 26:27-28)

Each of the apostles are invited – even commanded – to drink of the cup, binding them to this covenant.

In 1 Corinthians 11:25 Jesus' command extends beyond that special night: "Do this, whenever you drink it, in remembrance of me." While the text doesn't say so, I believe that whenever we celebrate the Lord's Supper we are sharing a Covenant Meal at Jesus' Table. We eat his Bread and drink his Wine, and so renew our commitment to the New Covenant he established so many years ago.

Q3. What is the significance of the 12 Apostles drinking the Cup of the Covenant? To whom would they correspond under the ratification of the Old Covenant? (Hint: Exodus 24:11.) What is the significance of *us* drinking the Cup of the Covenant?
http://www.joyfulheart.com/forums/index.php?showtopic=479

The Meal as Giving and Receiving Hospitality

Though it isn't part of the covenant aspects of the meal, it is useful to look at the Lord's Supper as a meal of close fellowship. In the ancient Near East, hospitality was a very high responsibility. When a stranger came to your home, you as host had a responsibility not only to offer him a meal, but to protect him while he was your guest. Examples are found in Abraham offering food to heavenly guests (Genesis 18:1-8) and Lot risking his life to defend them against enemies in Sodom (Genesis 19:1-8).

On the other hand, if you had received someone's hospitality, for you to seek to harm that person would be unthinkable. Judas' betrayal was especially heinous because he had received Jesus' hospitality and trust, but turned against him. Jesus said, "But this is to fulfill the scripture: 'He who shares my bread has lifted up his heel against me'" (John 13:18, quoting Psalm 41:9; cf. Matthew 26:23; Mark 14:10). Judas' treachery betrayed the trust of hospitality:

"Even my close friend, whom I trusted,
he who shared my bread,
has lifted up his heel against me." (Psalm 41:9)

"All your allies will force you to the border;
your friends will deceive and overpower you;
those who eat your bread will set a trap for you,
but you will not detect it." (Obadiah 1:7)

These verses represent the *negative*, the *breach* of the law of hospitality. But the *positive, the observance* is profound. Sharing a meal together was for those in the ancient Near East a powerful sign of a close bond with another person. It is twice used as a symbol of deep communion with God himself.

"You prepare a table before me
in the presence of my enemies.
You anoint my head with oil;
my cup overflows." (Psalm 23:5)

"Behold, I stand at the door and knock; if anyone hears My voice and opens the door, I will come in to him, and will dine with him, and he with Me." (Revelation 3:20)

Q4. Why is the Lord's Table such a time of intimate fellowship with Jesus? In your experience with having meals with friends, what makes the difference between a casual, forgettable meal, and one which is rich with memories? How can this insight make your experience of the Lord's Table more meaningful?
http://www.joyfulheart.com/forums/index.php?showtopic=480

Invitation to the Covenant

One of the most winsome passages in the entire Bible uses the metaphor of invitation to a fellowship meal with the idea of the covenant, which also echoes through the last book of the Bible (Revelation 21:6; 22:17):

"Ho! Every one who thirsts, come to the waters;
And you who have no money come, buy and eat.
Come, buy wine and milk
Without money and without cost.
"Why do you spend money for what is not bread,
And your wages for what does not satisfy?
Listen carefully to Me, and eat what is good,

And delight yourself in abundance.
"Incline your ear and come to Me.
Listen, that you may live;
✗ **And I will make an everlasting covenant** with you,
According to the faithful mercies shown to David." (Isaiah 55:1-3)

Jesus has offered that New Covenant, that everlasting covenant, to us, in the Cup signifying his blood shed on the cross. And he invites us to drink – first, each of the apostles:

"Drink from it, all of you." (Matthew 26:28)

and then each of us:

"This cup is the new covenant in my blood; do this, whenever you drink it, in remembrance of me." (1 Corinthians 11:25)

We are invited guests at Jesus' table where we share intimate table fellowship. And we are instructed to renew the covenant he has made with us on every occasion when we drink the Cup of the Lord. What an honor! What a privilege! What a joy!

"May the God of peace, who through **the blood of the eternal covenant** brought back from the dead our Lord Jesus, that great Shepherd of the sheep, equip you with everything good for doing his will, and may he work in us what is pleasing to him, through Jesus Christ, to whom be glory for ever and ever. Amen." (Hebrews 13:20-21)

Prayer

Father, when I think about the Covenant you've made with me I am overwhelmed. When I think about your love extended to me, I am amazed anew. Your heart's desire is to know me and love me intimately. May that be my true heart's desire towards You. In Jesus' holy name, I pray. Amen.

7. The Cup of Blessing and the One Loaf (1 Corinthians 10:16-17)

We've looked at this passage in Chapter 3. Now let's consider more completely two additional descriptions of the Lord's Supper – "the cup of blessing" and the "one loaf," both found in 1 Corinthians 10:16-17:

> "16Is not the cup of thanksgiving for which we give thanks a participation in the blood of Christ? And is not the bread that we break a participation in the body of Christ? 17Because there is one loaf, we, who are many, are one body, for we all partake of the one loaf." (1 Corinthians 10:16-17)

The Cup of Blessing

This phrase is translated two ways in modern translations:

> "The cup of blessing which we bless...." (KJV, NASB, NRSV)

> "The cup of thanksgiving for which we give thanks...." (NIV)

Detail of "The Institution of the Eucharist" (1640) by French Baroque painter Nicholas Poussin (1594-1665), oil on canvas, Musée du Louvre, Paris.

In this case, majority doesn't rule. Let me explain. A common understanding of the Greek words used here, *eulogia*, "blessing" and *eulogeō*, "to praise, bless," has been as "consecration" or "to consecrate," and conveys an idea perhaps carried over from the Lutheran and Roman Catholic understanding that the priest's prayer of consecration changes the bread and wine into Christ's actual body and blood.[1] With this understand-

---

[1] *Eulogeō*, BDAG 407-408, 2.b. So also Thayer 260.

ing the "cup of blessing which we bless" would mean "the cup that conveys blessing[2] which we consecrate...."

However, recent scholars are convinced that this misses entirely the context of the Jewish meals where blessings and thanksgivings were offered to God at the beginning and end of the meal (and, in the case of the Passover, during the meal). At the beginning of the meal, the first cup would prompt this blessing:

> "Blessed are You, O Lord our God,
> who have created the fruit of the vine."[3]

As Marshall puts it: "The cup of blessing was a Jewish technical term for the cup of wine, for which a blessing, i.e. thanksgiving, was given to God."[4] In the Passover Seder, the cup of blessing marked a common thanksgiving or praise for the food that occurred at the *conclusion* of the meal. The head of the house (or chief guest) would say, "Let us pronounce the blessing,"[5] followed by the simple blessing.[6] Jeremias, who has researched the ancient Jewish literature thoroughly, concludes that in the days of Jesus, the blessing at the conclusion of the meal probably had the following wording:

> "May You be praised, O Lord our God, King of the Universe, You who feed the whole world with goodness, grace, and mercy.

> We give thanks to You, O Lord our God, that you have caused us to take possession of a good and large land.

> Have mercy, O Lord our God, on Israel, Your people,
> and upon Your altar and upon Your temple.
> Praise be to You, O Lord, who builds Jerusalem." [7]

---

[2] *Eulogia*, BDAG 408-409, 3bβ.

[3] Edersheim, *Life and Times,* 2:496, with my editing to update the language from the "thee's and thou's." See also Alfred Edersheim, *The Temple: Its Ministry and Services as They Were at the Time of Christ* (Eerdmans, 1958, reprinted from 1874 edition), pp. 238-244.

[4] Marshall, *Last Supper and Lord's Supper,* p. 119-120. So also Jeremias, *Eucharistic Words,* p. 109, fn. 3; *Robertson's Word Pictures,* in loc., Vincent's *Word Studies,* in loc.; C. K. Barrett, *The First Epistle to the Corinthians* (Harper's New Testament Commentaries; Harper & Row, 1968).

[5] Hermann W. Beyer, *eulogeō, ktl.,* TDNT 2:754-765. He cites *jBer.,* 11 c f; *bBer.,* 51b; Strack and Billerback IV, 627ff. However, Beyer seems to see the verb in our verse as expressing blessing the congregation (2:763).

[6] Barrett, *1 Cor,* p. 231. Gordon D. Fee (*1 Corinthians,* pp. 467-468), says: "'Blessings' offered to the Creator for his bounty were a common part of Jewish meals. The 'cup of blessing' was the technical term for the final blessing offered at the end of the meal."

[7] Jeremias, *Eucharistic Words,* p. 111, citing L. Finkelstein, "The *Birkat ha-mazon,*" in *Jewish Quarterly Review,* new series 19 (1928-1929), 211-262.

The *Didache* or *Teaching of the Twelve Apostles*, a very early Christian document that dates to the end of the First Century AD, records the following thanksgiving to be used for the cup:

> "We thank You, our Father, for the holy vine of David your servant, which You made known to us through Jesus your Servant; to You be the glory for ever."

And for the broken bread:

> "We thank You, our Father, for the life and knowledge which You made known to us through Jesus your Servant; to You be the glory for ever. Even as this broken bread was scattered over the hills, and was gathered together and became one, so let your Church be gathered together from the ends of the earth into your kingdom; for yours is the glory and the power through Jesus Christ for ever."[8]

So the "cup of blessing" doesn't designate a cup that conveys blessings, but the phrase "cup of blessing" designates the cup that evokes blessing and thanksgiving towards God for all his blessings toward us, especially forgiveness of sin through the death of his Son.

To summarize, by "cup of blessing," Paul is referring to the "cup of thanksgiving (*eulogia*) for which we give thanks," with much the same meaning as "and when he had given thanks (*eucharisteō*), he broke it and said, 'This is my body...'" (1 Corinthians 11:24). Indeed, the early church referred to the Lord's Supper as both the Eucharist and the Eulogia, from these Greek words used to describe the prayers of thanksgiving offered by Jesus at the Last Supper.

Having clarified the actual meaning of the "cup of blessing," let me be quick to say that I acknowledge that the Lord's Supper conveys great blessings to those who partake. However, too often we partake of the Lord's Supper for our *own* blessing rather than as a service of worship and blessing towards *God*. We must take care not to be self-focused, but focused on Christ as we partake of the Lord's Supper. It is a feast of remembrance, of proclamation, of blessing God, and of thanksgiving towards him.

---

[8] *Didache* 9. Chapter 10 includes a prayer to be said after communion: " We thank You, holy Father, for your holy name which You did cause to tabernacle in our hearts, and for the knowledge and faith and immortality, which You madest known to us through Jesus your Servant; to You be the glory for ever. You, Master Almighty, did create all things for your name's sake; You gave food and drink to men for enjoyment, that they might give thanks to You; but to us You did freely give spiritual food and drink and life eternal through your Servant. Before all things we thank You that You are mighty; to You be the glory for ever. Remember, Lord, your Church, to deliver it from all evil and to make it perfect in your love, and gather it from the four winds, sanctified for your kingdom which you have prepared for it; for yours is the power and the glory for ever. Let grace come, and let this world pass away. Hosanna to the God (Son) of David! If any one is holy, let him come; if any one is not so, let him repent. Maranatha. Amen."

Q1. (1 Corinthians 10:16). What does the "cup of blessing" teach us about our focus at the Lord's Supper? Who is to be blessed when the "cup of blessing" is lifted heavenward?

http://www.joyfulheart.com/forums/index.php?showtopic=481

We Partake of the One Loaf (1 Corinthians 10:17)

We've considered the meaning of the "cup of blessing," now let us consider the special description of the bread in verse 17.

> "Because there is one loaf, we, who are many, are one body, for we all partake of the one loaf." (1 Corinthians 10:17)

The word "bread" (KJV, NRSV, NASB) or "loaf" (NIV) is the common word *artos*, "a baked product produced from a cereal grain, bread," also, "loaf of bread."[9]

Bread Making in Ancient Times

Making bread in ancient times was hard work. Of course, at harvest the wheat (or other grain) was cut, threshed (to separate the grain from the chaff or husks), winnowed (to remove the chaff from the grain), and gathered into a granary or storage container.

Bread was made in each home daily except on the Sabbath. A woman would have taken a measure of grain and then ground it by rubbing the grains between two portable grinding stones (Matthew 24:41). Then the flour was sifted. However, by Jesus' time large community, donkey-driven millstones were in use (Matthew 18:6) and have been found in Capernaum. They may have alleviated the work of grinding in each household. After the flour was made and sifted, water and salt were added and the dough was kneaded in a kneading-trough with a bit of the previous day's dough (which contained active yeast cells). Once the dough had been worked and the yeast distributed throughout the dough, it was put aside to rise. (Of course, during the Feast of Unleavened Bread and Passover, the yeast or leaven was omitted entirely to produced unleavened bread.)

After rising, the dough was shaped for baking. In America, we're used to fluffy bread baked in pans, but a round, thin loaf about 7 inches in diameter and perhaps 1/2 inches high was more typical in Jesus' day. Bread was baked in three ways:

---

[9] *Artos*, BDAG 136.

1. **"Ash bread"** was baked on hot stones from the fire, with ashes put over the dough to bake it. The bread was turned during baking. Jesus and his followers may have made this on campfires during their itinerant ministry.
2. A **pan or plate** of iron or pottery over the fire could be used, with perhaps some kind of lid to hold the heat in.
3. An **oven** was made of earth or clay in a round or cylindrical shape. The oven was heated with grass, stubble, thorns, or perhaps cow dung. After the fire had died down, the dough-cakes were stuck on the hot inside walls. The bread would not be turned, but removed from the oven when done. Bread baked in an oven was best – fairly thin and soft.[10]

Of course, the bread Jesus used at the Last Supper was unleavened, but we have no record that the early church made an effort to make special unleavened bread for the Lord's Supper. Their normal leavened bread was no doubt used for the occasion.

The One Loaf as a Symbol of Unity

It was the custom in Israel for the head of the house to begin each meal by taking the loaf of bread, giving thanks, and then breaking or tearing it and giving some to each one at the table. Among the disciples, Jesus was the one who broke the bread and began the meals this way. Paul uses this custom as a symbol of unity:

> "Because there is one loaf, we, who are many, are one body, for we all partake of the one loaf." (1 Corinthians 10:17)

The verse seems almost parenthetical to the main thrust of the passage. But Paul can't leave his mention of the bread without making a special point about unity. Why?

The Church at Corinth had serious problems with unity. Indeed, much of Paul's letter deals with issues that divided them and produced jealousy and quarreling (1 Corinthians 3:3). Some of the areas that divided them included:

1. **Allegiance to leaders.** Some claimed Paul as their mentor, others Apollos, or Cephas. Still others proclaimed that they followed Christ (1 Corinthians 1:10-13).
2. **Moral Issues.** They didn't have the unity they needed to disfellowship a member who was sleeping with his father's wife. Perhaps the immoral climate of Corinth made them resist godly standards of morality (5:1-13). Paul has to insist on stan-

---

[10] This section was based on information from Adrianus van Selms, "Bread," TDNT 1:540-544, and David M. Howard, Jr., "Oven," TDNT 3:622.

dards of morality with regard to sexual sins, as well as stealing, greediness, cheating in business, and slander (6:9-20)

3. **Religious Syncretism** (or mixing Christianity with idolatry). Some members felt it was okay to eat foods offered to idols, while others were consciousness-stricken (8:1-13). Still others attended the pagan services with their old friends and trade guild workers (10:6-33).

4. **Disputes between Members.** Members were openly suing each other in secular courts, rather than settling their differences by bringing them to the church (6:1-8).

5. **Class Distinctions.** At the common meals of the church community, the wealthy ate first without regard for the poor getting enough (11:17-22).

6. **Spiritual Gifts.** Spiritual gifts were a problem, with some flaunting their ability to speak in tongues while causing chaos in the church (Chapters 12 and 14). Paul had to emphasize the one Spirit who distributed the gifts to the one body (12:12-13).

7. **Doctrinal Disputes.** Some believe in the resurrection of Christ and others denied it (15:12ff).

Understood in this context, our verse must be seen as an attempt by Paul to use the symbol of the one loaf of bread to illustrate another metaphor of unity – Christian believers as a body with Christ as the head.

It's Me, O Lord

Dear friend, unity must begin with you and me, if it is to spread to others. We must examine our own hearts. We've all been hurt by others – sometimes intentionally, sometimes not. Against whom do we bear a grudge? (Mark 11:25). Who has something against you? (Matthew 5:23-24). Jesus says we must settle these things before we worship.

Q2. Read Mark 11:25 and Matthew 5:23-24. How do these relate to Paul's teaching on the One Loaf (1 Corinthians 10:17)? What must we personally do to achieve unity to prepare ourselves to partake of the Lord's Supper righteously?
http://www.joyfulheart.com/forums/index.php?showtopic=482

The Scandal of Christian Divisions

Paul speaks to our churches, too. Many churches – perhaps yours – are rent by divisions between members. Paul's message replicates Christ's high-priestly prayer to his Father on the evening of the Last Supper, "... that they may be one as we are one" (John 17:11). Indeed, for us to have credibility as Christians so that others might be attracted to Christ, we must put aside our divisions.

> "I give you a new commandment, that you love one another. Just as I have loved you, you also should love one another. By this everyone will know that you are my disciples, if you have love for one another." (John 13:34-35)

> "My prayer is not for them alone. I pray also for those who will believe in me through their message, that all of them may be one, Father, just as you are in me and I am in you. May they also be in us so that the world may believe that you have sent me." (John 17:20-21)

Many pastors refuse to deal with the mean-spirited, power-hungry, anger-driven members in their churches. Perhaps pastors won't deal with them because they know congregations will not back them up by insisting upon resolution of differences according to biblical principles (Matthew 18:15-20). Church discipline in our day is nearly dead and, as a result, churches are often undisciplined, sinful, carnal organizations that drive people away from Christ. Brothers and sisters, this must not be! We must confront disunity, as did Paul, or we will never see Jesus' command for mutual love and prayer for unity fulfilled in our congregations.

Q3. In what ways do the divisions in Corinth sound familiar in our own congregations? Don't pick on another congregation; how about your own? How serious was the need for unity? Can bickering congregations partake of the Lord's Supper without sin?
http://www.joyfulheart.com/forums/index.php?showtopic=483

But the problem in our day is not just *within* our congregations, but *between* our congregations. One of the scandals of Christendom is that the three Christian bodies that control holy sites in the Holy Land are constantly bickering. Of course, that is just a microcosm of the arrogance of our sectarian attitudes towards those in other Christian denominations. We have the gall to exclude Christian brothers and sisters from the

Lord's Table at our churches because we doubt the purity or authenticity of their faith, due to differences in their traditions from ours.

Pope John-Paul II set us all an example when he publicly confessed the sins of his Church and sought to reach out to both Protestants and Jews. His humility and love (however imperfect you may see it) were answered with a degree of reciprocal warmth. But when he reached out to the Orthodox churches, he was rebuffed by many. One ancient tradition cannot forgive the sins of another ancient tradition, even after a thousand years!

Too often, my beloved brothers and sisters, we cling to our own peculiar brand of doctrinal purity rather than to love that can bridge the differences between us. I'm not suggesting that we embrace sin or neglect doctrinal accuracy. We must maintain integrity. But even more important than our cherished interpretations is love for brothers and sisters who are just as sincere and devout as we. As a Protestant pastor I don't agree with all the practices or understandings of Catholics and Orthodox believers. But I must not be so filled with pride as to think that my supposed rightness is an excuse to be unloving. If we are one in Christ, then we must act like it, not in some kind of organizational unity so much as in a demonstration of the spiritual unity of all true believers in Jesus, regardless of tradition, nationality, and denomination.

Q4. (1 Corinthians 10:17) How does Paul's teaching on the One Loaf affect our relationships and love for those of other Christian denominations and traditions? How does blanket judgmentalism towards the faith of other Christian groups sometimes seem to excuse us from Jesus' command to love one another?
http://www.joyfulheart.com/forums/index.php?showtopic=484

Paul's words over the Lord's Supper to the divided Corinthians span the centuries to speak to us today:

> "Is not the cup of thanksgiving for which we give thanks a participation in the blood of Christ? And is not the bread that we break a participation in the body of Christ? Because there is one loaf, we, who are many, are one body, for we all partake of the one loaf." (1 Corinthians 10:16-17)

First, the Lord's Supper is an occasion of blessing God. It is a time of heartfelt thanksgiving for our salvation, at the awful cost of Christ's death. Second, the Lord's Supper must be a time of unity with our brothers and sisters. When we are alienated from one another, we must seek reconciliation, since we are "one body ... one loaf." Grant it, Lord Jesus!

Prayer

Father, as I read these two verses I sense your grief. So often I have partaken of the Lord's Supper selfishly, seeking my own blessing, not yours. Forgive me. So often we have been content to partake of your Bread while we excuse the divisions in our own congregation and between branches of your Church. Forgive us. Change our hearts, I pray that we might love you with all our hearts and our brothers as ourselves. Nothing less is enough. Forgive us. In Jesus' name, I pray. Amen.

8. Eating His Flesh, Drinking His Blood (John 6:53-57)

Of the four gospels, only the Gospel of John omits the Words of Institution of the Lord's Supper. But only John includes Jesus' extended teaching on Jesus as the Bread of Life (6:25-71). When he included it, I believe John knew that his readers would understand it in light of the Lord's Supper – these words especially:

Joos van Cleve (Dutch artist, 1485-1540), detail "The Last Supper," oil on wood, 45 x 206 cm, Musée du Louvre, Paris, Predella of "Altarpiece of the Lamentation" (c. 1530).

> "[53]Jesus said to them, "I tell you the truth, unless you eat the flesh of the Son of Man and drink his blood, you have no life in you. [54]Whoever eats my flesh and drinks my blood has eternal life, and I will raise him up at the last day. [55]For my flesh is real food and my blood is real drink. [56]Whoever eats my flesh and drinks my blood remains in me, and I in him. [57]Just as the living Father sent me and I live because of the Father, so the one who feeds on me will live because of me." (John 6:53-57)

This is an important passage to meditate on and understand, since it sheds light on the meaning of the Lord's Supper.

Context, Themes, and Parables

This is one of the more difficult passages in the New Testament, so don't be surprised if you're confused at first. To begin, let's consider the Bread of Life discourse (or teaching) as a whole.

Context: The Bread of Life discourse (6:25-71) was immediately preceded by Jesus' feeding of the 5000 (6:1-24), which prompted Jesus' followers to be interested in the concept of "bread." The discussion and the teaching that Jesus gave seem to begin at lakeside (6:25) and then continue on to teaching in synagogue in Capernaum (6:59).

Outline: This discourse can be divided into four general sections:

1. Jesus, the True Manna (6:27-34)
2. Jesus, the Bread of Life (6:35-51)
3. Partaking of the Son of Man (6:52-59)
4. Reactions to Jesus' Teaching (6:60-71)

But Jesus doesn't really use an outline. Rather this is a running dialog between Jesus and his hearers.

Themes: Throughout the discourse Jesus interweaves two related themes in and out. The first of these we'll be focusing on in this chapter:

1. **Believing on and continuing to trust in Jesus will bring a person to eternal life and ultimate resurrection in the Last Day** (6:39-40, 47, 57, 63, etc.).
2. But this is entirely from God, since **no one can come to Jesus unless the Father draws him, and Jesus will not lose any of them** (6:44-46, 65).

Metaphors or Parables: Jesus uses three parables or analogies or illustrations to teach these themes:

- **Manna**, "bread from heaven" (6:31-34, 38, 41-42, 49-50, 58)
- **Bread of Life**, that is, bread that brings about eternal life (6:35-42, 51, 58)
- **Flesh and blood** as "food" (6:51b-56)

These metaphors are related in that they all refer to eating and nourishing. These are the elements Jesus uses to weave a beautiful and powerful teaching on faith and eternal life.

1. Jesus, the True Manna (6:27-34)

In verses 27-29 Jesus establishes two things about salvation:

- The Son of Man (a title Jesus uses to refer to himself) will give you food that will sustain you not just for a few hours, but into the life to come (eternal life).
- We can't work for eternal life, we receive it by believing in Jesus.

Then he turns the discussion of manna from heaven to focus on the eternal life that he offers them:

"... it is my Father who gives you the true bread from heaven. For the bread of God is he who comes down from heaven and gives life to the world." (John 6:32b-33)

Jesus' hearers respond, "Sir, from now on give us this bread" (6:34), similar to the response of the Woman at the Well of Samaria: "Sir, give me this water so that I won't get thirsty and have to keep coming here to draw water" (John 4:15).

2. Jesus, the Bread of Life (6:35-51)

Now Jesus begins the first of the seven "I AM" passages in John (6:35; 8:12; 10:9; 10:11; 11:25; 14:6; 15:1). "I am" of course is a rather unveiled reference to the name by which God revealed himself to Moses as Yahweh – "I AM THAT I AM" (Exodus 3:14).

"35Then Jesus declared, '**I am the bread of life.** He who comes to me will never go hungry, and he who believes in me will never be thirsty. 36But as I told you, you have seen me and still you do not believe....'" (John 6:35-36)

In what way is Jesus like bread? His followers will never go hungry or be thirsty. Of course, he is speaking spiritually here, not physically, following the tradition of Isaiah 49:10 and 55:1-2. Jesus had used similar language with the woman at the well of Samaria:

"Everyone who drinks this water will be thirsty again, but whoever drinks the water I give him will never thirst. Indeed, the water I give him will become in him a spring of water welling up to eternal life." (John 4:13-14)

In John 6:35-51 Jesus teaches that:

- Faith in him results in the possession of eternal life right now! (6:47)
- Jesus is the Bread of Life, who, using the manna analogy, came down from heaven (6:51).
- The Bread of Life brings eternal life to those who eat it (6:50-51a).

So what does the metaphorical language "eating" the "Bread of Life" mean? Put verses 47 and 51a side by side and you can see clearly:
- verse 47: He who believes | has eternal life
- verse 51a: If anyone eats of this (living) bread | he will live forever

It's quite clear that "believing in Jesus" corresponds to "eating the Bread of Life," since these are used as parallel statements in the same context and with the same result – everlasting life. This theme weaves itself through this discourse, and is said first one way and then another throughout the passage (6:39-40, 47, 57, 63, etc.). St. Augustine put it this way: "For to believe on Him is to eat the living bread. He that believes eats; he is sated invisibly...."[1]

Q1. (John 6:35-51) What does the metaphor of "eating the Bread of Life" mean in practical terms? To extend the same metaphor, what do you think might be the difference between nibbling and actually making a meal of it?
http://www.joyfulheart.com/forums/index.php?showtopic=485

Flesh Given for the Life of the World (6:51b)

Jesus now moves from the analogy of the Bread of Life to a new analogy: the sacrifice of his body on the cross. This is the transition verse:

"This bread is my flesh, which I will give for the life of the world." (John 6:51b)

We've seen these words before in Chapters 1 and 4, but not put quite this way:
- "Flesh" (*sarx*) "body, physical body."[2]
- "Give, given" (*didōmi*) "to dedicate oneself for some purpose or cause, give up, sacrifice."[3]
- "For" (*hyper*) "in behalf of, for the sake of someone or something."[4]

The **purpose** of Jesus' gift of his body is "the life of the world," that is eternal life, the theme Jesus keeps coming back to in this passage. Now compare this verse in John to the Words of Institution in Luke:
- Luke 22:19b – "And he took **bread**, gave thanks and broke it, and gave it to them, saying, 'This is my body (*sōma*) **given** for you...'"
- John 6:51b – "This **bread** is my flesh (*sarx*) which I will **give** for the life of the world."

It's pretty clear to me that Jesus has the same thought in mind, even though these sayings were given at different times. Jesus' teaching on the Bread of Life serves as a kind of parallel teaching to the Words of Institution.

[1] Augustine, *Homilies on John*, 26, 1.
[2] *Sarx*, BDAG 914-916, 2a.
[3] *Didōmi*, BDAG 242, 10.
[4] *Hyper*, BDAG 1030-1031.

Q2. (John 6:51b) What is Jesus referring to when he says, "This bread is my flesh, which I will give for the life of the world"? What similarities do you see with Jesus' teaching at the Last Supper in Luke 22:19b?

http://www.joyfulheart.com/forums/index.php?showtopic=486

3. Partaking of the Son of Man (6:52-59)

Jesus' metaphor has now shifted from eating bread to eating flesh. There is an immediate reaction to Jesus' words, due to a revulsion in Judaism and most other cultures against cannibalism:[5]

> "[52]Then the Jews began to argue sharply among themselves, 'How can this man give us his flesh to eat?'
>
> [53]Jesus said to them, 'I tell you the truth, unless you eat the flesh of the Son of Man and drink his blood, you have no life in you. [54]Whoever eats my flesh and drinks my blood has eternal life, and I will raise him up at the last day. [55]For my flesh is real food and my blood is real drink. [56]Whoever eats my flesh and drinks my blood remains in me, and I in him. [57]Just as the living Father sent me and I live because of the Father, so the one who feeds on me will live because of me. [58]This is the bread that came down from heaven. Your forefathers ate manna and died, but he who feeds on this bread will live forever.' [59]He said this while teaching in the synagogue in Capernaum." (John 6:52-59)

The listeners take his words literally and are deeply offended, as Jesus undoubtedly knew they would be. But it seems as if Jesus purposely carries the idea farther yet, so that, if it is to be taken literally, it becomes more offensive yet.[6] Though some believe he is speaking literally of his own flesh and blood in the Eucharist, I see this as an example of Jesus' use of hyperbole to make his point powerful and unforgettable (Matthew 5:29-30; 19:24; Luke 6:41-42; 14:26; 1 Corinthians 9:27).

---

[5] For Jews to drink blood would have been morally repugnant because of the strong prohibitions against drinking blood (Genesis 9:3; Leviticus 7:26; 17:14; 19:26; Deuteronomy 14:4-5; Acts 15:29). Even the priests who partook of the flesh of the sacrifices in the tabernacle and temple didn't drink the blood. Though Jews could eat the meat of clean animals, to eat human flesh was especially repugnant to them (Talmud, *Chulin* 92b). The only times we hear of it in the Bible are during wartime sieges that mothers might eat their dead infants in order to keep from starving themselves (Leviticus 26:29; Deuteronomy 28:53-57; Isaiah 9:20; Lamentations 4:10; Ezekiel 5:10), and then with a sense of repugnance and revulsion.

[6] In verse 53, "eat" is the common Greek verb *esthiō*, "eat." In verse 54 a synonym is used, "eat," *trōgō* (also at John 13:18; Matthew 24:38), sometimes (though not here) used of animals feeding, "to bite or chew food, eat (audibly)"[6] (BDAG 1019).

Arguments for Taking the Passage Literally of the Eucharist

Let's examine arguments for taking this passage literally, of the Eucharistic flesh of Jesus. Nineteenth century German Catholic theologian Joseph Pohle says,

"Nothing hinders our interpreting the first part (6:26-48) metaphorically and understanding by 'bread of heaven' Christ Himself as the object of faith, to be received in a figurative sense as a spiritual food by the mouth of faith. Such a figurative explanation of the second part of the discourse (6:52-72), however, is not only unusual but absolutely impossible."[7]

Pohle's argument for impossibility, affirmed by the late Catholic New Testament scholar Raymond E. Brown,[8] is that since the metaphor for eating one's flesh is used as a metaphor for "hostile action" (Psalm 14:4; 27:2; 53:4; Zechariah 9:9) and drinking of blood was forbidden by God's law (Genesis 9:4; Leviticus 3:17; Deuteronomy 12:23; Acts 15:20)[9], therefore his words can't have a favorable meaning *unless* they refer to the Eucharist. However, it is clear to me that we are not required to go as far back as the Old Testament for the metaphor, just a few verses back where he speaks of eating the Bread of Life (6:50-51a). This is a continuation and intensification of that same metaphor.

On the other hand, Jesus clearly meant the Bread of Life portion of the discourse which preceded this to be taken figuratively. To take one section of the discourse figuratively and the other literally would be very strange indeed, especially since Jesus sums it up in verse 58 with a reference back to his previous words about the Bread of Life:

"This is the bread that came down from heaven. Your forefathers ate manna and died, but he who feeds on this bread will live forever." (6:58)

What Does Jesus Mean about Eating His Flesh, Drinking His Blood?

If this is figurative language, as I believe it is, then what is Jesus saying? Observe in 6:53-59 the consequences of eating Jesus' flesh and drinking his blood. Let's look at these verse by verse, examining the consequence as well as similar sayings elsewhere:

[7] Joseph Pohle, "Real Presence of Christ in the Eucharist," *Catholic Encyclopedia* (Robert Appleton Company, 1909; Online edition ©2003 by K. Knight), vol. V. Dr. Pohle, a professor of dogmatic theology, was an influential author of the late nineteenth and early twentieth centuries.

[8] Brown, *John* 1:284-285. Brown's second argument for taking this passage literally as regarding the Eucharist is: "It is possible that we have preserved in 6:51 the Johannine form of the words of institution." This is speculative at best, as evidenced by his words, "it is possible."

1. **6:53 – "Having life in oneself."** The consequence of believing is to have life in his name, according to John 20:31. In 1 John 5:10-12, having life is associated with believing in the Son of God.

2. **6:54a – "Has eternal life."** Eternal life is the consequence of believing in John 6:40a, as well as in John 3:15-16; 3:36; 5:24; 1 Timothy 1:16; 1 John 5:13; etc.

3. **6:54b – "Resurrection on the last day."** Resurrection on the last day is the consequence of believing according to John 6:40b. Jesus also connects believing in him with resurrection and eternal life in the raising of Lazarus (John 11:25-26)

4. **6:56 – "Remains or abides in Jesus."** This is also a consequence of believing Jesus' words according to John 15:7. His word remaining or abiding in us is connected with eternal life (1 John 2:23-25), being true disciples (John 8:31-32), and bearing fruit (John 15:5).

5. **6:57 – "Live because of me."** The consequence of believing in the "I am the resurrection and the life" passage, John 11:25-26.

6. **6:58 – "Live forever."** This is the consequence of eating of the "living bread" in John 6:51b above. It is another way of saying one "has eternal life" (see 6:54a above). In John 11:26 Jesus connects believing in him with never dying.

It is pretty clear that the consequences of putting one's faith in Jesus – believing in Jesus – are the same as "eating his flesh and drinking his blood." This is a strong, even *extreme*, metaphor for faith.[9] As F.F. Bruce puts it: "To believe in Christ is not only to give credence to what he says; it is to be united to him by faith, to participate in his life."[10]

4. Reactions to the Teaching (6:60-71)

The metaphor was so vivid, so extreme, in fact, that it caused an uproar. Many "disciples" left and no longer followed Jesus. Here is an example of the secrets of the

---

[9] Other Bible references to drinking blood are Isaiah 49:26 and Revelation 16:16.

[10] F.F. Bruce, *The Hard Sayings of Jesus* (InterVarsity Press, 1983), p. 21. St. Augustine (354-430) gave guidelines on how to determine whether an expression is to be taken literally or figuratively. On 6:63 he comments: "If the sentence is one of command, either forbidding a crime or vice, or enjoining an act of prudence or benevolence, it is not figurative. If, however, it seems to enjoin a crime or vice, or to forbid an act of prudence or benevolence, it is figurative. 'Except ye eat the flesh of the Son of man,' says Christ, 'and drink His blood, ye have no life in you.' This seems to enjoin a crime or a vice; it is therefore a figure, enjoining that we should have a share in the sufferings of our Lord, and that we should retain a sweet and profitable memory of the fact that His flesh was wounded and crucified for us" (*On Christian Doctrine*, III, 16, 24).

Kingdom being given in parables to reveal the truth to true disciples and obscure it from those who follow the crowds only (Mark 4:11-12).

In this passage also, Peter voices the faith of the Twelve:

> "Lord, to whom shall we go? You have the words of eternal life. We believe and know that you are the Holy One of God.'" (John 6:68-69)

It is striking to me that this defection by many disciples is an illustration of Jesus' teaching about belief:

> "To the Jews who had believed him, Jesus said, 'If you hold to my teaching, you are really my disciples. Then you will know the truth, and the truth will set you free.'" (John 8:31-32)

There are some "hard sayings" in life that cause the faint of heart to let go. There are those who assent to Jesus' words, but when there is a crisis of faith, those who *continue to feed* on Jesus, who continue to believe, who abide in him, are his true disciples; the others walk away. This entire passage is about Jesus having "the words of eternal life," that is, the words, which, when believed, result in eternal life.

Q3. (John 6:53-71) If to eat Jesus' flesh and drink his blood is a strong expression for "to believe," why does Jesus emphasize this so strongly? What was the difference between the Twelve and the crowd of "disciples" that turned away from Jesus? What is the mark of true disciples according to John 8:31-32?
http://www.joyfulheart.com/forums/index.php?showtopic=487

The Spirit Gives Life, the Flesh Counts for Nothing (6:63)

Jesus continues:

> "The Spirit gives life; the flesh counts for nothing. The words I have spoken to you are spirit and they are life." (John 6:63)

There has been lots of controversy about the exact meaning of this verse. The central question is what does "flesh" (*sarx*) refer to?

1. The most natural reference would be back to Jesus' previous paragraph – eating his flesh and drinking his blood. If we take "eating my flesh" figuratively as "believing in Jesus," as I have argued, the meaning would be: **The Spirit give life, believing in me counts for nothing**. But that doesn't make any sense. This is rather a contrast between Spirit and flesh.

2. If we take "eating my flesh" literally of the Eucharist, the meaning would be: **The Spirit gives life, eating the sacramental flesh counts for nothing.** Zwingli argued along this line against Luther's view of the Real Presence. But this assumes that Jesus in this discourse in Capernaum was speaking directly concerning the Lord's Supper which would take place later, an assumption we just don't have evidence to make.

3. More likely then, Jesus is not referring to the flesh of 6:53-56, but rather contrasting flesh and Spirit, much as he did in his discussion with Nicodemus in John 3:6: "That which is born of the flesh is flesh; and that which is born of the Spirit is spirit." In this case "flesh" would mean, "the natural principle in man which cannot give eternal life."[11] So the meaning of Jesus' words in 6:63 is probably: **The Spirit gives life; what man can understand and achieve on his own counts for nothing. The words I have spoken to you – spiritually discerned and believed – bring spiritual life, eternal life.**

The Bread of Life Passage and the Lord's Supper

As indicated earlier, while I don't believe Jesus deliberately gave this teaching with reference to the Sacrament of the Eucharist, I do believe that St. John, as he composed the Fourth Gospel, included this discourse knowing that his readers would read it with the Lord's Supper in mind. The Bread of Life passage and the Lord's Supper have parallel teachings.

The Lord's Supper deliberately uses elements intended to remind us of Jesus' body and blood: chewy bread to remind us of flesh, red wine to remind us of blood. The act of partaking of the Lord's Supper certainly is one of feeding on Jesus – a physical symbolic act that speaks of a much deeper communion indeed:

- To feed on the Bread of Life is to believe Jesus' words and trust in him as the source of our life.
- To eat Jesus' flesh and blood means to utterly depend upon him and the truths he teaches for sustenance and life itself.

When we partake of the Lord's Supper we are commanded to remember Jesus' death for our sins. Our mind also turns to the Spirit of God that raised him from the dead, the same Spirit that gives us spiritual life to us and will ultimately raise our bodies from the

---

[11] So Brown, *John* 1:300.

dead on the Last Day. The Lord's Supper as an act of remembering, reflecting, believing, trusting – this indeed reenergizes us as food to our souls and life to our faith. As the Anglican service directs as the bread is given to the recipient:

> "Take and eat this in remembrance that Christ died for thee, and feed on him in thy heart by faith, with thanksgiving."

Feeding on Jesus' words and basking in his presence are the essence of trust, of true belief in him. Yes, partake of his body and blood in the Lord's Supper as a sign that you indeed feed on him in your heart – and so grow in your faith. Amen.

Q4. How does "eating the Bread of Life" (to use Jesus' metaphor in John 6) nourish our faith? How does partaking of the Lord's Supper build and nourish our faith? What does the main point of the Bread of Life discourse (John 6:25-69) have in common with "Do this in remembrance of me," in Jesus' Words of Institution (1 Corinthians 11:23-26)?
http://www.joyfulheart.com/forums/index.php?showtopic=488

Prayer

Father, so often my devotional life seems dry. Sometimes I partake of the Lord's Supper without really thinking too much about what I am doing. Forgive me. Teach me to truly feed on Jesus in my heart by faith, with thanksgiving. Help me to become less dependent upon my own ways, but wholly dependent upon Him, wholly trusting, wholly walking by faith. In Jesus' name, I pray. Amen.

9. The Lord's Supper and the Great Banquet (Luke 22:16, 18; Matthew 26:29)

"I tell you, I will not drink of this fruit of the vine from now on **until that day when I drink it anew with you in my Father's kingdom.**" (Matthew 26:29 || Mark 14:25)

Pieter Brueghel, "The Peasant Wedding" (1568), oil on canvas, 124 x 164 cm, Museum of Art History, Vienna, Austria.

"14When the hour came, Jesus and his apostles reclined at the table. 15And he said to them, 'I have eagerly desired to eat this Passover with you before I suffer. 16For I tell you, I will not eat it again **until it finds fulfillment in the kingdom of God.**' 17After taking the cup, he gave thanks and said, 'Take this and divide it among you. 18For I tell you I will not drink again of the fruit of the vine **until the kingdom of God comes.**' (Luke 22:16-18)

"For whenever you eat this bread and drink this cup, you proclaim the Lord's death **until he comes.**" (1 Corinthians 11:26)

In each of the Synoptic Gospels and in 1 Corinthians 11, the Words of Institution look forward to a fulfillment in the future. A key element in our own celebration of the Lord's Supper is future-looking, as well. Let's explore this.

Jewish Expectation of the Great Feast

An expectation of the Great Feast on the Last Day began perhaps with a wonderful prophecy from Isaiah, clearly eschatological, that is, speaking of the Last Days:

"On this mountain the LORD Almighty will prepare
a **feast of rich food for all peoples**,
a banquet of aged wine–
the best of meats and the finest of wines.
On this mountain he will destroy
the shroud that enfolds all peoples,
the sheet that covers all nations;

> he will swallow up death forever.
> The Sovereign LORD will wipe away the tears
> from all faces;
> he will remove the disgrace of his people
> from all the earth." (Isaiah 25:6-8)

You find echoes of this prophecy in the Old Testament and the New, finally being fulfilled in Revelation with the Marriage Supper of the Lamb (Revelation 19:6-9) and the New Heavens and the New Earth (Revelation 21:4).

It's pretty clear from the Bible and from Jewish rabbinical literature that – at least the Pharisees in Jesus' time – had a strong expectation of this Great Feast after the resurrection:

> "Blessed is the man who will eat at the **feast** in the kingdom of God," (Luke 14:15) – comment by a dinner companion

> Yahweh will **recline at table**, the patriarchs and the righteous at His feet,[1] and "They will recline at table and eat in Gan Eden."[2] – rabbinical commentary on Exodus

> "At the last coming he will lead out Adam and the patriarchs and bring them (into the paradise of Eden) that they may rejoice, as when a man invites his friends to eat with him, and they come and speak with one another before the palace, joyously awaiting his **feast**, the enjoyment of good things, of immeasurable wealth and joy and happiness in light and everlasting life."[3] – pseudepigraphical Book of Enoch

> "Rise and stand, and see at the **feast** of the Lord the number of those who have been sealed." – Old Testament Apocrypha, 2 Esdras 2:38

> "The **feast** of our God, which He will prepare for the righteous, has no end."[4] – Midrash on Esther

Jesus' Teaching on the Great Banquet

It was in this context that Jesus taught. He often alluded to the Great Feast in the Kingdom of God, both in parables and in direct comments. For example:

---

[1] *Exodus rabba* 25 on 16:4, cited by Rudolf Meyer, *kolpos*, TDNT 3:824-826, fn. 8.

[2] *Exodus rabba*, 25 on 16:4, in Strack and Billerback IV, 1148, cited by Johannes Behm, *esthiō*, TDNT 2:689–695.

[3] *Slavic Enoch* 42:5 Cited by Johannes Behm, *deipnon*, TDNT 1:35. Also, "The Lord of spirits will dwell over them, and they will eat and lie down and rise up to all eternity with that Son of Man," *Ethiopian Enoch* 62:14 Cited by Johannes Behm, *deipnon*, TDNT 1:35.

[4] *Midrash Esther* 1, 4 Cited by Johannes Behm, *deipnon*, TDNT 1:35. In *Pesikta rabbati*, 41, a collection of homilies, where Jacob is invited to the feast of redemption (Strack and Billerback, IV, 1154; I, 878f. Cited by Johannes Behm, *deipnon*, TDNT 1:35).

Parable of the Great Banquet. At a dinner to which Jesus was invited he told his not to invite those who could invite him back, so that he would be rewarded "at the resurrection of the righteous" (Luke 14:14). One of the guests remarked: "Blessed is the man who will eat at the feast in the kingdom of God" (Luke 14:15). Jesus followed with the Parable of the Great Banquet (Luke 14:18-24, partial parallel in Matthew 22:2-14), the point of which was that the Jews (who had been invited to the banquet but made excuses) would be displaced by the Gentiles.

Reward for the Apostles. "And I confer on you a kingdom, just as my Father conferred one on me, so that you may **eat and drink at my table** in my kingdom and sit on thrones, judging the twelve tribes of Israel." (Luke 22:29-30)

Teachings on Inclusion and Exclusion. "People will come from east and west and north and south, and will take their places at the **feast** in the kingdom of God." (Luke 13:29-30 || Matthew 8:11)

Parable of the Delayed Householder. "It will be good for those servants whose master finds them watching when he comes. I tell you the truth, he will dress himself to serve, will have them recline at the table and will come and wait on them." (Luke 12:37)

Parable of the Ten Virgins. "And while they went to buy, the bridegroom came, and those who were ready went in with him to the marriage feast; and the door was shut."[5] (Matthew 25:10)

Parable of the Rich Man and Lazarus. "The time came when the beggar died and the angels carried him to Abraham's side...." (Luke 16:22). Being in Abraham's bosom pictures both a place of honor and a place of loving, intimate fellowship.[6]

Gathering the Elect. The elect are gathered at Christ's coming for this very feast. "And he will send his angels and gather his elect from the four winds, from the ends of the earth to the ends of the heavens." (Mark 13:27 || Matthew 24:31)

Q1. Why are so many of Jesus' teachings oriented toward the future? What kinds of associations come to mind as you think of the Great Banquet?
http://www.joyfulheart.com/forums/index.php?showtopic=489

---

[5] "Entry into the kingdom, whether a door is mentioned (Matt. 25:10) or not, usually implies entry into the festive hall for the eschatological banquet (Matt. 7:7-8; 22:12; 25:10, 21ff.; Luke 13:24-25; 14:23)" (Joachim Jeremias, TDNT 3:173-180).

[6] Rudolf Meyer, *kolpos*, TDNT 3:824-826; Gustav Stählin, *agapaō*, TDNT 9:113–171.

The Marriage Supper of the Lamb

The Book of Revelation also refers to the Great Banquet. In a promise to overcomers in his letter to the churches, Jesus says:

> "He who has an ear, let him hear what the Spirit says to the churches. To him who overcomes, I will give the right to eat from the tree of life, which is in the paradise of God" (Revelation 2:7)

Revelation culminates with the Marriage Supper of the Lamb:

> "Then I heard what sounded like a great multitude, like the roar of rushing waters and like loud peals of thunder, shouting:
>
> > 'Hallelujah!
> > For our Lord God Almighty reigns.
> > Let us rejoice and be glad
> > and give him glory!
> > For the wedding of the Lamb has come,
> > and his bride has made herself ready.
> > Fine linen, bright and clean,
> > was given her to wear.'
>
> (Fine linen stands for the righteous acts of the saints.)
>
> Then the angel said to me, 'Write: "Blessed are those who are invited to the wedding supper of the Lamb! "' And he added, 'These are the true words of God.'" (Revelation 19:6-9)

The Lord's Supper Looks Forward to the Great Banquet

With this introduction, you can now appreciate Jesus' words on that last night:

> "I tell you, I will not drink of this fruit of the vine from now on **until that day when I drink it anew with you in my Father's kingdom**." (Matthew 26:29 || Mark 14:25)

> "For I tell you, I will not eat it again until it finds **fulfillment** in the kingdom of God." (Luke 22:16)

"Fulfillment" is the verb *plēroō*, "to make full." Here it could have one of two meanings: "to bring to a designed end, fulfill" a prophecy, a promise, etc., or "to bring to completion an activity in which one has been involved from its beginning, complete, finish."[7] Indeed, the Lord's Supper is *fulfilled* at the Great Banquet. This gathering of the redeemed of the Lord in the presence of God on the Last Day is the culmination and fulfillment of the incarnation, the cross, and the resurrection.

---

[7] *Plēroō*, BDAG 828-829, 4.a or 5. Gerhard Delling, *plērēs, ktl.*, TDNT 6:283-311.

Q2. (Luke 22:16) In what sense does the Lord's Supper find its "fulfillment" in the Great Banquet at the end of the age? What should this do to our thoughts at the Lord's Table?

http://www.joyfulheart.com/forums/index.php?showtopic=490

The Promise of Future Fellowship

I'm saddened by the many Christians who, for one reason or another, no longer attend church. The church is flawed, they've been hurt in the church, the church is filled with hypocrites, and so forth. *And these things are too often true!* But we are not to give up on Christian fellowship.

> "Let us not give up meeting together, as some are in the habit of doing, but let us encourage one another – and all the more as you see the Day approaching." (Hebrews 10:25)

For in our future is a seat at the Great Banquet with millions of other fellow believers. Isn't it ironic that we would separate ourselves now from those with whom we'll share the Feast and an eternity in heaven? The essence of a banquet – and of the Lord's Supper – is not food on which to gorge ourselves, but the joyful fellowship of those at the table.

The Lord's Supper as a Promise of the Future

The Lord's Supper is our reminder that this life isn't "as good as it gets." Just as the seal of Holy Spirit is your guarantee of future glory (Ephesians 1:13; Romans 8:23; 2 Corinthians 1:22), so the piece of bread and portion of wine you hold in your hands are a token of your ticket to the Great Banquet at the end of the age.

The Lord's Supper looks *backward* as a *remembrance* to the death of Christ for our sins. It looks to the *present* as a *communion* with the living Christ, and it looks to the *future* as a *promise of eternal life* in the presence of God.

Q3. In what sense does the Lord's Supper point to the past? How does it point to the present? How does it point to the future?

http://www.joyfulheart.com/forums/index.php?showtopic=491

We Shall See His Face

As I think about that Great Banquet, I begin to look forward to it afresh, for it will be the time of "entering into the joy of our Lord." The chorus of an old gospel hymn comes to mind:

"O I want to see Him, look upon His face,
There to sing forever of His saving grace;
On the streets of glory let me lift my voice,
Cares all past, home at last, ever to rejoice."[8]

On that day, the promise of Revelation will be realized. Jesus told his disciples that despite various appearances in one form or another, "No one has seen God at any time" (John 1:18; 1 John 4:12), that is, his essential Spirit-nature. But on that Day, the scripture says,

"They will see his face, and his name will be on their foreheads. There will be no more night. They will not need the light of a lamp or the light of the sun, for the Lord God will give them light. And they will reign for ever and ever." (Revelation 22:4-5)

"I tell you, I will not drink of this fruit of the vine from now on **until that day when I drink it anew with you in my Father's kingdom**." (Matthew 26:29)

Q4. (Revelation 22:4) When you meditate on "seeing his face," what thoughts come to mind? Why should the Lord's Supper stimulate these thoughts every time we partake of it?
http://www.joyfulheart.com/forums/index.php?showtopic=492

Prayer

Father, so often our minds are focused on our own needs and problems. Henceforth, may the Lord's Supper turn our eyes instead to the Great Banquet and the culmination of all things in you. Maranatha. Come soon, Lord Jesus! Amen.

---

[8] "O I Want to See Him," words and music by Rufus H. Cornelius (1916). Another gospel song on this theme is "All Things Are Ready, Come to the Feast," words by Charles H. Gabriel (1895), music by William A. Ogden.

10. Preparing Ourselves for the Lord's Supper (1 Corinthians 11: 27-34)

The Apostle Paul makes it clear that it is possible to approach the Lord's Table in an "unworthy manner." Just what does this mean? How can we prepare ourselves to partake of the Lord's Supper?

Sieger Köder (German priest-artist, 1925-), "The Last Supper." The painting is from the perspective of Christ facing his disciples. You see Jesus' face reflected in the cup of red wine, the Chi Rho symbol in the broken bread, the cross, etc.

"27Therefore, whoever eats the bread or drinks the cup of the Lord in an unworthy manner will be guilty of sinning against the body and blood of the Lord. 28A man ought to examine himself before he eats of the bread and drinks of the cup. 29For anyone who eats and drinks without recognizing the body of the Lord eats and drinks judgment on himself. 30That is why many among you are weak and sick, and a number of you have fallen asleep. 31But if we judged ourselves, we would not come under judgment. 32When we are judged by the Lord, we are being disciplined so that we will not be condemned with the world. 33So then, my brothers, when you come together to eat, wait for each other. 34If anyone is hungry, he should eat at home, so that when you meet together it may not result in judgment. And when I come I will give further directions." (1 Corinthians 11:27-34)

Before we consider eating and drinking unworthily, let's survey the context of Paul's teaching.

Divisions between the Rich and Poor in Corinth (11:17-22)

The church at Corinth had various problems with unity, with divides between pastoral allegiance (1 Corinthians 1:12; 3:1-10), spiritual gifts (1 Corinthians 12-14), and in our passage, economic status. Apparently, people in the early church often brought their own food to meetings of the congregation, which would likely have met in the larger homes of the wealthy members. They would eat an Agape Meal together, mixing a communal meal with a celebration of the Lord's Supper. Verses 17-22 give us the situation:

> "[17]In the following directives I have no praise for you, for your meetings do more harm than good. [18]In the first place, I hear that when you come together as a church, there are divisions among you, and to some extent I believe it. [19]No doubt there have to be differences among you to show which of you have God's approval. [20]When you come together, it is not the Lord's Supper you eat, [21]for as you eat, each of you goes ahead without waiting for anybody else. One remains hungry, another gets drunk. [22]Don't you have homes to eat and drink in? Or do you despise the church of God and humiliate those who have nothing? What shall I say to you? Shall I praise you for this? Certainly not!" (1 Corinthians 11:17-22)

The problem in Corinth was that the rich would go ahead and eat without waiting for others – and not even making sure that the poor in the congregation had eaten or even brought food with them. The poor probably made up a large portion of the congregation, many of them slaves (1 Corinthians 7:21-23).

The class divisions in the society at large remained in the church. By eating without the poor, the rich showed utter disdain for their brothers and sisters. It was more than rudeness. It was an offence against Christian unity.

Paul had confronted church divisions before. Once he had rebuked the Apostle St. Peter who had eaten with Gentiles in Antioch, but separated himself from them when Jewish Christians came from Jerusalem – trying to show them that he was a good Jew who didn't eat with Gentiles (Galatians 2:11-14). At the conclusion of his first letter to the Corinthian church Paul tells them:

> "The body is a unit, though it is made up of many parts; and though all its parts are many, they form one body. So it is with Christ. For we were all baptized by one Spirit into one body – whether **Jews or Greeks, slave or free** – and we were all given the one Spirit to drink." (1 Corinthians 12:12-13)

Paul is disgusted at the behavior of the wealthy Corinthian church members. You can catch his tone in the words: "What shall I say to you? Shall I praise you for this? Certainly not!" (1 Corinthians 11:22).

Not Discerning the Body (11:29)

Following this rebuke, Paul gives instructions on the Words of Institution of the Lord's Supper (11:23-26), which we have considered in detail before. Then he returns to implications of the wealthy members' disregard for the poor. Rather than going through this passage verse by verse, let's begin our exploration with verse 29, since it holds the key to Paul's meaning:

> "For anyone who eats and drinks without recognizing the body [of the Lord] eats and drinks judgment on himself." (1 Corinthians 11:29, NIV)

"Discerning" (KJV, NRSV) or "recognizing" (NIV, NJB) is *dokimazō*, "to make a critical examination of something to determine genuineness, put to the test, examine," often used of assaying the genuineness of metal.[1] Fee sees the meaning here as "to discern, distinguish as distinct and different."[2] But to understand this verse we must determine what Paul means by "the body." There is a textual variant here. The NIV and KJV render the phrase "the Lord's body." But the earliest Greek manuscripts (followed by the NRSV, NASB, NJB, etc.) omit "the Lord's," which was probably included by an early copyist to help explain the word "body."[3]

I see two possible interpretations of the word "body":

1. **"Body" refers to the Eucharistic elements**, that is, the bread and wine which represent Christ's body and blood. The meaning is thus that the communicants – that is, those taking communion – are judged for not recognizing that they are partaking of a sacred meal, and must act accordingly towards one another, caring for the needs of the poor and those who come in late.
2. **"Body" refers to the church, the "Body of Christ."** The meaning is thus that communicants are judged for not discerning needs of other members the Body of Christ, that is, the congregation.

---

[1] *Dokimazō*, BDAG 255-256. Walter Grundmann, *dokimos*, TDNT 2:255-260.

[2] Fee, *1 Corinthians*, p. 564.

[3] The earliest Greek manuscripts omit "the Lord's," including p46 Aleph* B C* 33 1739 cop^sa,bo etc. Later manuscripts include it: Aleph2 D F G K P Ψ most miniscules it syr^p,h,pal goth arm etc. The United Bible Societies committee give it a {C} degree of certainty ({A} is highest, {D} is lowest). Metzger (*Textual Commentary*, p. 562-563) argues for the "shorter reading" saying, "there appears to be no good reason to account for the omission if the words had been present originally."

The main argument for "body" as the Eucharistic elements is that the most immediate uses of the word "body" are clearly referring to the Eucharistic bread representing Christ's flesh. "Body" here serves a kind of "shorthand" for "body and blood."[4]

The main argument for "body" as the church is that references to "body" in the immediate passage are to "body and blood" together, not to "body" by itself. There is a clear reference to "body" as the church in 1 Corinthians 10:17 – "Because there is one loaf, we, who are many, are one body, for we all partake of the one loaf." Since verse 16 clearly uses "body" in a Eucharistic sense, we know that Paul can freely mix these metaphors within the same topic.[5] Of these two interpretations, I see the second as more likely.

Paul contends that partaking of the Lord's Supper without making sure that other members of the congregation are taken care of is "unworthy." The Greek *anaxiōs* means "in an unworthy/careless manner."[6] To partake in such a fashion is to live lower than their calling to "walk worthy of the gospel" (Philippians 1:27; 1 Thessalonians 2:12; Colossians 1:10; Ephesians 4:1; 3 John 6).

Sinning against the Body and Blood of the Lord (1 Corinthians 11:27)

What does it mean to sin "against the body and blood of the Lord" (verse 27). It means to commit an act that is disrespectful of this holy meal, in this case, by eating of it in a careless fashion, without a thought of slighting others in the congregation. The Lord's Table, as it is called in 1 Corinthians 10:21, is holy and demands our reverence. If we sin carelessly and then expect to partake of the elements depicting Christ's suffering and death for our sins, we are hypocrites. In the Old Testament, the priests had become casual towards holy things and were rebuked for it:

> "You place defiled food on my altar.
> But you ask, 'How have we defiled you?'
> By saying that the LORD's table is contemptible." (Malachi 1:7)

As terrible as it is to sin "against the body and blood of the Lord," however, realize that it is no more or less sinful than other sins against fellow Christians. For example,

---

[4] Barrett (*1 Corinthians*, p. 275) concludes, "Though the verse remains problematical and uncertain, it is best, in view of the parallelism between verses 27 and 29 ... to interpret 'the body' (29) in light of 'the body and blood of the Lord' (27), which is now taken up in shorthand form." Leon Morris (*1 Corinthians*, p. 164) agrees.

[5] Fee (*1 Corinthians*, pp. 562-564) argues this position convincingly. Bruce (*1 & 2 Cor.*, p. 115) seems to adopt this interpretation.

[6] *Anaxiōs*, BDAG 69. This is a compound word *a-* "not" + *axios*, "pertaining to having a relatively high degree of comparable worth or value, corresponding, comparable, worthy, fit, deserving" (BDAG 93-94).

Paul admonishes those who flaunt their so called "freedom" in Christ in a way that offends or scandalizes weaker Christians, "When you sin against your brothers in this way and wound their weak conscience, you sin against Christ" (1 Corinthians 8:12). Jesus spoke in a similar way in the Parable of the Sheep and the Goats (Matthew 25:31-46) where neglecting "one of the least of these brothers of mine" was like a sin against Jesus himself.

Q1. (11:29) Why does "not discerning the body" at the Lord's Supper constitute such a grave sin? Aren't there worse things a church could have done?
http://www.joyfulheart.com/forums/index.php?showtopic=493

Incurring Judgment and Discipline (1 Corinthians 11:29-32)

Paul warns the Corinthians that to continue sinning is to invite punishment. Two words are used to describe this punishment:

- **"Judgment"** (NIV, NRSV, NKJV) or **"damnation"** (KJV) in verse 29 is *krima*, "legal decision rendered by a judge, judicial verdict."[7]
- **"Disciplined"** (NIV, NRSV) or **"chastened"** (KJV) in verse 32 is *paideuō*, "to assist in the development of a person's ability to make appropriate choices, practice discipline," here, to discipline with punishment,[8] especially the kind of punishment a parent might give to a child to help mold his or her character.

Paul is not talking here about eternal damnation for the sinning Corinthians (as suggested by the KJV translation), but corrective punishment, "that we should not be condemned[9] with the world." The writer of Hebrews reminds us (quoting from Proverbs 3:11-12):

> "'My son, do not make light of the Lord's discipline,
> and do not lose heart when he rebukes you,
> because the Lord disciplines those he loves,
> and he punishes everyone he accepts as a son.'

---

[7] *Krima*, BDAG 567, 4b.
[8] *Paideuō*, BDAG 2 bα.
[9] *Katakrinō*, "pronounce a sentence after determination of guilt" (BDAG 519).

> Endure hardship as discipline; God is treating you as sons. For what son is not discip-
> lined by his father?" (Hebrews 12:5-7)

Nevertheless, this discipline can be severe if we resist it, resulting in sickness or even premature death.

> "That is why many among you are weak and sick, and a number of you have fallen asleep." (1 Corinthians 11:30)

We may think this is too harsh of God. He should be more forgiving! we cry. Our problem is that we minimize the seriousness of sin. We excuse ourselves and then wonder why God won't. God our Father is seeking to form us in his own image. We also maximize death as the ultimate penalty, whereas for his children, God sees it as a homecoming, not eternal death. He will deal with our sins if we won't, but he prefers that we recognize ourselves what needs to be done and repent without him applying pressure.

Q2. (1 Corinthians 11:29-32) Why has God brought judgment to the offending parties at Corinth? Isn't sickness and death rather harsh? How does God's discipline actually work for our good in the light of Hebrews 12:5-7?
http://www.joyfulheart.com/forums/index.php?showtopic=494

Self-Examination (1 Corinthians 11:28, 31)

Paul recommends that take heed to this ourselves. He uses two words to describe this:

"Examine" yourself (verse 28), *dokimazō* (which we saw as "discerning" or "recogniz-ing" in verse 29) "to make a critical examination of something to determine genuineness, put to the test, examine."[10]

> "A man ("person," *anthropos*) ought to examine himself before he eats of the bread and drinks of the cup" (verse 28)

"Judge" yourself (vs. 31), *diakrinō*, used twice in this passage to mean, "to evaluate by paying careful attention to, evaluate, judge." In verse 31 it is used as "evaluate oneself." In verse 29 it means "recognize" the body.[11]

> "But if we **judged ourselves**, we would not come under judgment." (verse 31)

---

[10] *Dokimazō*, BDAG 255-256.
[11] *Diakrinō*, BDAG 231.

In two other passages Paul urges self-examination:

> "Examine yourselves (*peirazō*[12]) to see whether you are in the faith; test (*dokimazō*) yourselves." (2 Corinthians 13:5)

> "Each one should test (*dokimazō*) his own actions. Then he can take pride in himself, without comparing himself to somebody else, for each one should carry his own load." (Galatians 6:4-5)

Q3. (1 Corinthians 11:28, 31) Introspection by a neurotic person can foster guilt and self-loathing. Where is the balance? How can we conduct self-examination and self-judgment so that it has a healthy rather than an unhealthy result in us?
http://www.joyfulheart.com/forums/index.php?showtopic=495

Confession and Repentance

Jesus, too, encouraged reflection when we come to worship God. Here are a pair of verses – one from Matthew, one from Mark – that serve as the flip side of each other:

> "Therefore, if you are offering your gift at the altar and there remember that your brother has something against you, leave your gift there in front of the altar. First go and be reconciled to your brother; then come and offer your gift." (Matthew 5:23-24)

> "And when you stand praying, if you hold anything against anyone, forgive him, so that your Father in heaven may forgive you your sins." (Mark 11:25)

The *Didache*, a late first-century Christian document, says in the context of the Lord's Supper:

> " But every Lord's day gather yourselves together, and break bread, and give thanksgiving after having confessed your transgressions, that your sacrifice may be pure. But let no one who is at odds with his fellow come together with you, until they be reconciled, that your sacrifice may not be profaned..."[13] (*Didache* 14.2)

It is significant that the 12 Steps of Alcoholics Anonymous includes these steps:

   4.   "Made a searching and fearless moral inventory of ourselves.

---

[12] *Peirazō*, "to endeavor to discover the nature or character of something by testing, put to the test" (BDAG 792-793).

[13] Bruce notes that the last phrase is a possible reference to the sacrifice referred to in Matthew 5:23-24 cited above (*1 & 2 Cor.*, p. 115).

5.   Admitted to God, to ourselves and to another human being the exact nature of our wrongs.
6.   Were entirely ready to have God remove all these defects of character.
7.   Humbly asked Him to remove our shortcomings.
8.   Made a list of all persons we had harmed, and became willing to make amends to them all.
9.   Made direct amends to such people wherever possible, except when to do so would injure them or others."

(Were you aware that the 12 Steps were developed by evangelical Christians?) It is one thing to acknowledge a sin. It is another to repent of it as wrong and seek to make it right, if possible.

For many centuries the Roman Catholic Church has required regular confession to a priest as a prerequisite to taking communion. Done sincerely, confession can aid in spiritual growth and victory over sin. Protestants have often taken sin much too lightly. In the context of sickness resulting from unacknowledged sin, St. James exhorts confession and repentance, so there might be healing (James 5:16).

Confession to another human, such as an accountability partner, is a powerful way of helping us deal squarely with our sins. But we can also confess our sins to God alone and receive forgiveness (absolution) of our sins (1 John 1:9; Psalm 32:5; 51:2-5). No matter how confession is made, confession and repentance are absolutely necessary to growth in the Christian life. When we bury our sins, we stagnate, falter, and are subject to our Father's loving but firm discipline.

If we know we are living with unrepented sin, is it more respectful of Jesus not to partake of the Lord's Supper? Yes, it is more respectful, but it is stupid. We are subject to God's discipline for hanging onto sin whether or not we take communion. There is a time to repent and come clean, and let the chips fall where they will. The Lord's Supper is a reminder to us that *now* is the time to examine ourselves, *this* is the day to get back on the path. Paul writes:

> "As God's fellow workers we urge you not to receive God's grace in vain... I tell you, *now* is the time of God's favor, *now* is the day of salvation." (2 Corinthians 6:1)

Q4. How do confession and repentance fit with self-examination? What is the result of self-examination without confession and repentance? How do confession and repentance serve to bring spiritual health and character change?
http://www.joyfulheart.com/forums/index.php?showtopic=496

How to Prepare for Communion

Of course, we should begin each day in reflection, confession, and repentance. But especially when we come to the Lord's Table it is a time to "do business with God." How do we prepare ourselves for communion?

1. If possible, **take some time before the communion service**, at home or arriving at church early. Don't expect the pastor or the liturgy to do this preparation for you. Fellowshipping with others at church is good, but not if it distracts you from that heart-preparation necessary so that you can worship God aright.
2. **Examine yourself to see if you are in sin**, either a known sin or perhaps something you are unaware of. This means to pause to consider your life. How are you treating the people close to you? How are you treating those in the congregation? With indifference? With selfishness? With disrespect?
3. **Confess any sins**, known sin or sins that God brings to mind as you are examining yourself.
4. **Repent of these sins** and resolve to take immediate steps to correct your actions or make amends, if you are able.
5. **Accept God's forgiveness**. This time of self-reflection and repentance is not to give Satan permission to continually beat you up over sins of the past. Accept and believe in God's promises of forgiveness. We don't look backward – our sins have been forgiven. We look forward to living with God the day ahead of us.

Occasionally we can undo a wrong, but many times we cannot, and to try to do so might be harmful to others and seem self-serving. Sometimes we must resolve not to sin like that again, accept God's forgiveness, and go on, trusting his promise that he will "forgive our sins and purify us from all unrighteousness" (1 John 1:9).

We have examined in some detail the Words of Institution,

> "This is my body, which is for you; do this in remembrance of me.... This cup is the new covenant in my blood; do this, whenever you drink it, in remembrance of me." (1 Corinthians 11:24-25)

But just to understand it isn't enough. Now we are called to live our lives before God with thanksgiving for his sacrifice and humble appreciation for his forgiveness. The Lord's Supper is designed by our Lord to both nourish us and cause us to grow in him.

My prayer for both you and me is that Jesus' intention for his Supper might be fulfilled in us, in our congregations, and in our world – now and until Jesus' return in glory.

> "For whenever you eat this bread and drink this cup, you proclaim the Lord's death until he comes" (1 Corinthians 11:26).

Prayer

Father, forgive me for the times that I've come to the Table without preparing my heart to commune with you. Help me and my brothers and sisters to come to you ready to give worship and receive your blessings of the Word and the refreshing Holy Spirit. We love you, but we are weak; help us. In Jesus' name, we pray. Amen.

Appendix 1: A Brief Glossary of the Lord's Supper

If you've only partaken of the Lord's Supper in one or two congregations, you're probably ignorant of the many words used by different traditions. One term is not "better" than another, just different. Some of these words I have used in this book are as follows:

Words for the Lord's Supper

Lord's Supper is used directly in 1 Corinthians 11:20 to describe this ceremony of remembrance. This word is common in most denominations. The term **Last Supper** refers to the historical event which took place the day before Jesus' crucifixion at which he instituted or began the practice of the Lord's Supper.

Communion, from Latin *communion-*, *communio*, "mutual participation," from *communis*. The Latin Vulgate translates the Greek word *koinōnia* in 1 Corinthians 10:16 this way. The King James Version (KJV) translates *koinōnia* as "communion" here also. This idea of mutual sharing has come into English as "communion," and emphasizes both the way

Juan de Juanes (Spanish painter, 1523-1579), "Christ with the Chalice," wood, 101 x 63 cm, Museum of Fine Arts, Budapest. Jesus is holding the "host" in this painting.

that the Lord's Supper unites God's people and the communion we have with Christ at the Table. This word is very common among Protestant groups, such as Methodists, Presbyterians, Baptists, and others, and is often referred to as Holy Communion.

Eucharist, from Greek *eucharisteō*, "be thankful," comes from the account that Jesus "gave thanks" (Matthew 26:27, Mark 14:23, Luke 22:19, 1 Corinthians 11:24) before presenting to his followers the bread and the wine. This word is more common in liturgical churches such as Roman Catholic, Anglican, and Episcopal.

Mass is used by Roman Catholics, Anglo-Catholics, and some High Church Lutherans to refer to the service of the Lord's Supper. The word comes from Vulgar Latin *messa*, literally, "dismissal at the end of a religious service," and Late Latin, "to send." A related word **missal** is a book containing all that is said or sung at mass during the entire year.

Maundy Thursday refers to the day on which the Lord's Supper took place, which some churches celebrate with a Maundy Thursday service. Maundy comes from the Latin *mandatum*, "command" from which we get our English word "mandate." That night Jesus said, "A new command I give you: Love one another. As I have loved you, so you must love one another" (John 13:34).

Agape Feast or **Love Feast** is another term in Scripture for the Lord's Supper (Jude 12), used especially these days by the House Church movement. *Agapē* is the Greek word most often used to describe "selfless love." Generally an Agape Feast refers to a full meal that Christians have together, during which the bread and wine are eaten, such as was the practice in Corinth and the early church (1 Corinthians 11:20-22; Acts 2:46; Jude 12).

The Breaking of Bread (Acts 2:42, 46; 20:7) is another way the early church referred to the Lord's Supper.

Divine Liturgy is the term often used by the Byzantine tradition – Eastern Orthodox, Oriental Orthodox, and some Eastern-Rite Catholic churches. The word "liturgy" comes from Greek *leitourgia*, "public service." In English it refers to a rite or body of rites prescribed for public worship. **Holy Qurbana**, or "**Holy Sacrifice**" is the term used by the Chaldean and Syriac Christian Rites. **Badarak** is the term in the Armenian Church.

Host is a term sometimes used to describe a small, thin, round wafer used for communion, especially by those who believe in transubstantiation (see below). The word comes from Latin *hostia*, "victim, sacrificial animal," and is used in the Roman Catholic tradition and occasionally by Anglicans.

Chalice, from the Latin *calix*, "cup," is a goblet intended for drinking during a ceremony.

Cup is the term used in the New Testament to refer the drinking vessel (and often the wine contained within the vessel) used in the Lord's Supper (Matthew 26:27; Mark 14:23; Luke 22:20; 1 Corinthians 10:16, 21; 11:25-26).

Table of the Lord (1 Corinthians 10:21) is another way of referring to the Lord's Supper, emphasizing the host who invites people to a meal in his presence, fulfilled in heaven (Luke 22:30). In the Old Testament the term "Lord's table" referred to the priesthood's ministry of sacrifice and offering (Malachi 1:7, 12).

Nouns Used to Refer to the Lord's Supper

What should we call this action of partaking of the Lord's Supper? There are several terms used to describe this kind of religious act:

Sacrament (from Latin *sacrare*, "to consecrate"), is probably the most common term, defined in the dictionary as, "a Christian rite (as baptism or the Eucharist) that is believed to have been ordained by Christ and that is held to be a means of divine grace or to be a sign or symbol of a spiritual reality." Catholics recognize seven sacraments (Eucharist, baptism, ordination, penance, confession, marriage, and last rite). Most Protestants recognize two sacraments (the Lord's Supper and baptism).

Ordinance (from Latin *ordinare*, "to set in order, appoint"[4]), "a prescribed usage, practice, or ceremony." Sometimes this word is used instead of sacrament by those who want to deemphasize what they would consider "magical" ideas that have been associated with the term "sacrament." They use ordinance to emphasize Christ's direct command and usually restrict the term "ordinance" to the Lord's Supper or baptism.

Rite and Ritual (from Latin *ritus*, "number") is a more general term meaning in this context, "a prescribed form or manner governing the words or actions for a ceremony; the ceremonial practices of a church or group of churches." The Lord's Supper can properly be referred to as an ordinance, a sacrament, or a rite, depending upon your tradition. Some Christians use the term "ritual" with a bit of contempt, but if you observe them, they come to use the same prescribed words again and again, such as wedding vows or words at the Lord's Table.

Rites and rituals are not wrong. They are human ways in which we reverently set apart certain events as special, as sacred. Being critical of other Christians' rites and traditions shows our own narrowness, parochialism, and critical spirit more than the supposed purity of our doctrine or the superiority of our freedom in Christ.

The Presence of Christ in the Sacrament

Transubstantiation. (trans- = "change") The miraculous change by which, according to Roman Catholic and Eastern Orthodox dogma, the Eucharistic elements at their consecration become the body and blood of Christ while keeping only the appearances of bread and wine.

Sacramental Union (sometimes called Consubstantiation, con- = "same"). The actual substantial presence and combination of the body and blood of Christ with the Eucharistic bread and wine according to a teaching associated with Martin Luther.

Real Presence. Catholics believe in the *corporeal presence* or *Real Presence* of Christ in the sacrament, that the bread becomes Christ's body, and that when they partake they are taking in Christ's actual body.

Celebrate, Perform, Partake

While we're at it, let's clarify the *verbs* that describe the Lord's Supper in our day. Different traditions use different verbs. I share this so you'll be able to understand when other Christians relate the Lord's Supper in their own tradition and so you won't be offended by their terminology.

Celebrate, in this context, means "to perform (a sacrament or solemn ceremony) publicly and with appropriate rites," such as in "celebrate the mass." Some Protestants use "celebrate" to mean to praise God with joy and exuberance. Don't confuse this connotation with "celebrate" in connection with the Lord's Supper. That's really a different and separate use of the word. The person who officiates at the Lord's Supper is technically referred to as the "celebrant."

Perform, in this context, means "to do in a formal manner or according to a prescribed ritual."

Partake of, as in the phrase, "partake of the Lord's Supper," means to eat and drink the communion elements.

Enact, to act out. In a sense we act out the Last Supper, breaking the bread, offering prayers and blessings, and distributing the elements to those present.

Appendix 2: A Brief History of the Doctrine of the Real Presence and Transubstantiation

This is a Bible study, not a doctrinal treatise. However, since the position of the Early Church Fathers is used by some to support the doctrine of the Real Presence, I've outlined its historical development.

The doctrine of the Real Presence, that is, that Christ is present corporeally (i.e. bodily) in the sacrament of the Lord's Supper, has a long history in the Western Church, culminating in the Roman Catholic teaching of transubstantiation and Luther's view of sacramental union.[1] However, the Real Presence wasn't taught in the earliest times.

Paul's language "the body and blood of the Lord" in reference to eating the Lord's Supper unworthily (1 Corinthians 11:27), of course, was very early, though most Protestants would contend that he was speaking figuratively, not literally.

Hans Holbein the Younger (1497-1543), The Last Supper (1524-25), Limewood, 115,5 x 97,3 cm, Kunstmuseum, Öffentliche Kunstsammlung, Basle.

---

[1] Note: I am tracing here only beliefs in the Real Presence and transubstantiation, not other Catholic understandings of the Lord Supper, such as the Eucharist being an offering or sacrifice or the adoration of the consecrated elements.

The Early Church Fathers

A survey of the early Church Fathers indicates that the earliest documents and Fathers such as the *Didache* (late first century)[2] and Justin Martyr (died c. 165)[3] don't assert the doctrine of the Real Presence of Christ in the sacrament. Ignatius of Antioch (died by 117) comes closer when he protested of his Gnostic opponents that

> "They do not admit that the Eucharist is the flesh of our Savior Jesus Christ, the flesh which suffered for our sins and which the Father, in His graciousness, raised from the dead."[4]

However, by the time of Irenaeus (died c. 200 AD), you find statements that the bread and wine are strictly Christ's body and blood, in an argument against the Docetists about the reality of Christ's earthly body.[5] Tertullian (died c. 220 AD) and Cyprian (died 258 AD) sometimes used terms that indicate a symbolic understanding of the body and blood. Kelly concludes, however, that

> "While accepting the equation of the elements with the body and blood, [Tertullian] remains conscious of the sacramental distinction between them."[6]

Symbolic Vocabulary

Though the trend was to see the communion elements as the actual body and blood of Christ, there is another strain as well that used a symbolic vocabulary to refer to the elements of the Lord's Supper. Serapion (died 211 AD) refers to the elements as "a likeness."[7]

Eusebius of Caesarea (died c. 339 AD) on the one hand declares, "We are continually fed with the Savior's body, we continually participate in the Lamb's blood." However, he also writes that Christians daily commemorate Jesus' sacrifice "with the symbols of his body and saving blood," and that he instructed his disciples to make "the image of his own body," and to employ bread as its symbol.[8]

---

[2] *Didache* 9:1-5; 10:3; 14:1-3.
[3] Justin Martyr, *Dialogue with Trypho* 41:3.
[4] Ignatius, *Letter to the Smyrnaeans*, 6.
[5] Irenaeus, *Romans* 7:3; *Smyrna* 6f. Cited by Kelly, *Doctrines*, pp. 196-198.
[6] Kelly, pp. 211-216.
[7] Kelly, p. 441, cites Serapion, *Euchol.* 13, 12-14.
[8] Cited by Kelly, p. 441, *De solemn. pasch.* 7.

The *Apostolical Constitutions* (compiled c. 380 AD) use words such as "antitypes" and "symbols" to describe the elements, though they speak of communion as the body of Christ and the blood of Christ.[9]

Other Fathers who mix Real Presence vocabulary with symbolic terms include Cyril of Jerusalem (died 444),[10] Gregory of Nazianzus (died 389),[11] and Macarius of Egypt (died c. 390 AD).[12]

Athanasius clearly distinguishes the visible bread and wine from the spiritual nourishment they convey.[13] The symbolic language did not point to absent realities, but were accepted as signs of realities which were present but apprehended by faith.[14]

While St. Augustine (died 430) can be quoted to support various views of the Lord's Supper, he apparently accepted the widespread realism theory of his time,[15] though in some passages he clearly describes the Lord's Supper as a spiritual eating and drinking.[16]

An Open Controversy

However, the uses of symbolic language cited above are exceptions. More and more the more popular, vividly materialistic theory was adopted that regarded the elements as being converted into the Lord's body and blood.

Though the Latin church had been moving toward the view of the Real Presence for some time, the first person who clearly taught the doctrine of transubstantiation (though not using that term) was Paschasius Radbertus (785-865), abbot of the monastery at Corbey, France, in a book *On the Body and Blood of the Lord* (831 AD). His chief opponent among several was Ratramnus, another monk at Corbey, who wrote a tract asserting a sacramental rather than literal sense in which the elements were the body and blood of Christ.[17] Radbertus was later canonized as a saint and Ratramnus' book banned by the Roman Church.

---

[9] *Apostolical Constitutions* 5, 14, 7; 6, 23, 5; 7, 25, 4.

[10] Cited by Kelly, p. 441, Cyril of Jerusalem, *Cat.* 22, 9; 23, 20; 22, 3.

[11] Cited by Kelly, p. 441, Gregory of Nazianzus, *Or.* 45, 19; 8, 18.

[12] Cited by Kelly, p. 441, Marcarius of Egypt, *Hom.* 27, 17.

[13] Athanasius, *Ad. Serap.* 4, 19.

[14] Examples such as these of symbolic language in the early Church Fathers are given less importance by J. Pohle, "The Real Presence of Christ in the Eucharist," *Catholic Encyclopedia* (1908 edition).

[15] Kelly, pp. 446-448.

[16] Cited by Kelly, pp. 446-448, Augustine, *Enarr. in ps.* 3, 1; 98, 9; *Serm.* 131, 1; *tract. in ev. Ioh.* 27, 5; 25, 12; 26, 1.

[17] Philip Schaff, *History of the Christian Church*, vol. 4, §126-127.

In reaction to Radbertus' assertion of the corporeal presence of Christ in the Eucharist, Berengar (d. 1088) defended Ratramnus openly, but when threatened with trial and excommunication recanted. By the mid-eleventh century, transubstantiation was a dogma of the Latin church and was officially accepted in the Fourth Lateran Council (1215).[18]

The Reformers on the Real Presence

Several centuries later Martin Luther challenged the doctrine of transubstantiation and contended for a belief that the Real Presence was present "under, through, and with" the communion elements. He called this "sacramental union," though some have termed it "consubstantiation." Luther affirms the Real Presence in his Smaller Catechism:

> "Q. 287. What does Christ give us in this sacrament?
>
> In this sacrament Christ gives us His own true body and blood for the forgiveness of sins.
>
> Q. 288. How does the Bible make it clear that these words of Christ are not picture language?
>
> Christ's words in the Sacrament must be taken at face value especially because: A. these words are the words of a testament, and even an ordinary person's last will and testament may not be changed once that person has died; B. God's Word clearly teaches that in the Sacrament the bread and wine are a communion or participation in the body and blood of Christ; C. God's Word clearly teaches that those who misuse the Sacrament sin not against bread and wine but against Christ's body and blood."[19]

Luther's view of the Real Presence was opposed by Swiss theologian Zwingli at the Colloquy of Marburg. Most Protestants other than Lutherans, however, have followed the view of John Calvin who affirmed a spiritual presence of Christ with those who partake of communion. A typical Calvinistic formulation of the spiritual presence is found the Westminster Shorter Catechism (1647).

> "The Lord's supper is a sacrament, wherein, by giving and receiving bread and wine, according to Christ's appointment, his death is showed forth; and the worthy receivers are, not after a corporal and carnal manner, but by faith, made partakers of his body and blood, with all his benefits, to their spiritual nourishment, and growth in grace."[20]

---

[18] Ibid., vol. 4, §128-130.

[19] *Luther's Smaller Catechism*, questions 287-288.

[20] *Westminster Shorter Catechism*, Question 96: What is the Lord's Supper? Developed out of the English Reformation by English and Scottish divines in the 1647.

Appendix 3: Songs, Choruses, and Hymns for Communion

One way to enrich your experience of the Lord's Supper is to sing songs designed for communion. Many songs about the cross, Christ's sacrifice for sins, and communing with Jesus are appropriate. But here are specific communion songs, arbitrarily divided into newer and older songs. Many of these, especially the older ones, have the lyrics available online. As you meditate, read out loud some of these wonderful poems of Eucharistic worship.

Fifth century mosaic of "Loaves and Fishes" from the floor of an ancient church and monastery at Tabgha, on the north shore of the Sea of Galilee, near where Jesus is said to have fed the 5,000, thus initiating his Bread of Life discourse.

Newer Communion Songs

Most of the words and tunes can be found in the Song Select feature of Christian Copyright Licensing International (CCLI, www.ccli.com).

At This Table, words and music by Allan Robert Petker (©1990, 1992 Descant Publishing, Admin. by Fred Bock Music Company, Inc.)

Broken and Spilled Out, by Bill George and Gloria Gaither (©1984 William J. Gaither, Inc., Gaither Copyright Management, Yellow House Music)

Broken for You, words and music by Jack Hayford (©1980 Pilot Point Music, Lillenas, Admin. by The Copyright Company)

Come As You Are, words and music by Brent Helming; (© 1996 Maranatha Praise, Inc.)

Come Expecting Jesus, by John Chisum and Nancy Gordon (© 1996 Integrity's Hosanna! Music Mother's Heart Music, Admin. by ROM Administration)

Come to the Table, by Claire Cloninger and Martin J. Nystrom (©1991 Integrity's Hosanna! Music, Word Music, LLC, a div. of Word Music Group, Inc.)

Come, Share the Lord, words and music by Bryan Jeffery Leech (© 1984, Fred Bock Music Co., in *Chalice Hymnal*, 1995)

Commune With Me, by Kirk Dearman (© 1981 Maranatha Praise, Inc./Word Music, Inc.)

Communion Song, words and music by Barry McGuire (©1977 Sparrow Song, a div. of EMI Christian Music Publishing)

Communion Song, words and music by John Michael Talbot (©1979 Birdwing Music, Admin. by EMI Christian Music Publishing) |

Eat This Bread, words and music by Jacques Berthier (GIA Publications)

From Every Race, from Every Clime, words by Thomas B. McDormand (1974), music: Latvian Folk Melody (in *New Broadman Hymnal*, 1977)

Hungry, I Come, words and music by Craig Curry (©2002, Fred Bock Music Company)

I Am the Bread of Life, words and music by John Michael Talbot (©1982, Birdwing Music, Admin. by EMI Christian Music Publishing)

I Am the Bread of Life, words and music by Suzanne Toolan (©1971, GIA Publications, in *The Hymnal 1982*, The Episcopal Church)

I'm Gonna Eat at the Welcome Table, words and music, African-American spiritual (arrangement © 1980 G. Shirmer, Inc., in *Chalice Hymnal*, 1995)

In Remembrance of Me (Cheri Keaggy; 1996, Sparrow Song)

In Remembrance of Me, words by Ragan Courtney, music by Burylk Red (© 1972, Broadman Press; assigned to Van Ness Press, Inc., in *Chalice Hymnal*, 1995)

Jesus, Stand Among Us, words and music by Graham Kendrick (©1977, Thankyou Music, Admin. by EMI Christian Music Publishing)

Let us Break Bread Together on Our Knees, words and music African-American spiritual

Now the Silence, words by Jaroslav Vajda, music by Carl Schalk (© 1969, Hope Publishing Company)

One Bread, One Body, words and music by John B. Foley (© 1978 by John B. Foley, S.J., and New Dawn Music, in *Chalice Hymnal*, 1995)

Our Blessing Cup (John Michael Talbot; 1982 Birdwing Music/BMG Songs, Inc.)

Remember Me, by David Ritter and Jared Ming (© 1998 New Spring)

Remember Me, by Gerrit Gustafson and Martin Nystrom (©1990 Integrity's Hosanna! Music)

Seed, Scattered and Sown, words and music by Dan Feiten (© 1987, Ekklesia Music, Inc., in *Chalice Hymnal*, 1995)

The Bread of Life for All Men Broken, words by Timothy T'ing-fang Lew (1936), translated by Walter R.O. Taylor (1943), music by Su Yin-Lan (1934, in *New Broadman Hymnal*, 1977)

There's a Table in Your Presence, by Gary Sadler and Lynn DeShazo (© 2005 Integrity's Hosanna! Music Paintbrush Music, Admin. by Paintbrush Music)

This Is My Body, words and music by Jack Hayford (© 1980 Pilot Point Music)

Thy Supper, Lord, Before Us Spread, words by Joseph F. Green (1961), music by Irving Wolfe (© 1961, 1964, Broadman Press, in *New Broadman Hymnal*, 1977)

We Break This Bread, words and music by Chris Rolinson (©1980, 1987, 1999 Thankyou Music, Admin. by EMI Christian Music Publishing, The Central Board of Finance of the Church of England; The Archbishops' Council)

We Remember You, words and music by Kirk Dearman (©1988 Maranatha Praise, Inc., Admin. by Music Services)

We Remember You, words and music by Nancy Lowry (©1995, New Spring, Imagenuity Songs, Admin. by Music Services)

We Will Meet You There, by Jeff Slaughter and John Chisum (© 1994 Integrity's Hosanna! Music)

We Will Remember, by Gary Sadler and Lynn DeShazo (©1997 Integrity's Hosanna! Music)

What the Lord Has Done In Me, words and music by Reuben Morgan (©1998 Reuben Morgan, Hillsong)

When You Do This, Remember Me, words by Alexander Campbell (19th century), adapted with music by David L. Edwards (©1988, David L. Edwards, in *Chalice Hymnal*, 1995)

Where Can We Find Thee, Lord, So Near, words by Thomas B. McDormand (1974), tune: Federal Street, Henry K. Oliver (1832, in *New Broadman Hymnal*, 1977)

Older Communion Hymns

Most of the words and tunes (as MIDI files) are available on Hymntime.org and Oremus Hymnal (www.oremus.org/hymnal)

According to Thy Gracious Word, words by James Montgomery (1825), music by Hugh Wilson (1800)

Beneath the Forms of Outward Rite, words by James A. Blaisdell (1867-1957), music by William Gardiner, or by Luther O. Emerson (1866)

Blest/Sweet Feast of Love Divine, words by Edward Denny (1839), music by George F. Handel, or by Hans G. Nägeli (1773-1836).

Bread of Heaven, on Thee We Feed, words by Josiah Conder (1824), various tunes (in *The Hymnal 1982*, The Episcopal Church)

Bread of the World in Mercy Broken, words by Reginald Heber (1827), music by John S. B. Hodges (1868)

Break Thou the Bread of Life, words by Mary A. Lathbury (1877), music by William F. Sherwin (1877)

Come, Risen Lord, and Deign to be Our Guest, words by George Wallace Briggs (1941), music *Sursum Corda* by Alfred Morton Smith (1941), (words ©1941, Oxford University Press, in *The Hymnal 1982*, The Episcopal Church)

Come with Us, O Blessed Jesus, words by John Henry Hopkins, Jr. (1872), music Johann Schop (1665) (in *The Hymnal 1982*, The Episcopal Church)

Completed, Lord, the Holy Mysteries, words from the Liturgy of St. Basil, translated by Cyril E. Pocknee (1906-1980), music: Song 4 (in *The Hymnal 1982*, The Episcopal Church)

Deck Thyself, My Soul, with Gladness, words by Johann Franck (1649), translated from German by Catherine Winkworth (1858), music Schmücke Dich by Johann Crüger (1649)

Draw Nigh and Take the Body of the Lord, words from the *Antiphonarium Benchorense*, a late 7th century manuscript from the Monastery of Bangor, Ireland, translated from Latin to English by John M. Neale (1851), various tunes (in *The Hymnal 1982*, The Episcopal Church)

Father, We Thank Thee Who Hast Planted, words translated from Greek *Didache* (ca. 110 AD), by F. Bland Tucker (1941), music: *Rendz a Dieu*, Louis Bourgeois (in *The Hymnal 1982*, The Episcopal Church)

For the Bread, Which Thou Hast Broken, words by Louis F. Benson (1924), music by Charles J. Dickinson (1822-1883)

From the Table Now Retiring, words by John Rowe, music by Isaac B. Woodbury

Here at Thy Table, Lord, We Meet, words by Samuel Stennett (1727-1795), music by Hugh Wilson

Here at Thy Table, Lord (this sacred hour....), words by May Pierpont Hoyt (19th century), music by William F. Sherwin (1877, same tune as "Break Thou the Bread of Life")

Here, O My Lord, I See Thee Face to Face, words by Horatius Bonar (1855), music by Felix Mendelssohn, or by James Langran (1861)

Humbly I Adore Thee, Verity Unseen, words by St. Thomas Aquinas (ca. 1260), translated The Monastic Diurnal (1932), music *Adoro devote*, French church melody (1697; in *The Hymnal 1982*, The Episcopal Church)

In Memory of the Saviour's Love (... we keep the sacred feast), words by Thomas Cotterill (1805), music adapted from Johann M. Haydn, or "St. Peter" by Alexander R. Reinagle (1836)

Let Thy Blood in Mercy Poured, words translated from Greek by John Brownlie (1907), music Johann Crüger (1653, in *The Hymnal 1982*, The Episcopal Church)

Lord of Our Highest Love, words by Gilbert Young Tickle (1819-1888), music by W. H. Havergal, founded on a melody by J.B. König, "Franconia", 1738)

Lord, at Thy Table We Behold, words by Joseph Stennett (1727-1795), music by Lowell Mason

My God, Thy Table Now Is Spread, words by Philip Doddridge (1755), tune: Rockingham (1780; in *The Hymnal 1982*, The Episcopal Church)

Now, My Tongue, the Mystery Telling, words by St. Thomas Aquinas (13th century), translated from Latin by Edward Caswall (1861), various tunes (in *The Hymnal 1982*, The Episcopal Church)

O Food to Pilgrims Given, words in Latin (1661) translated by John Athelstan Laurie Riley (1906), various tunes (in *The Hymnal 1982*, The Episcopal Church)

O God, Unseen Yet Ever Near, words by Edward Osler (1836), music St. Flavian (1562) (in *The Hymnal 1982*, The Episcopal Church)

O Thou, Who at Thy Eucharist Didst Pray (that all thy Church might be forever one....), words by William Harry Turton (1881), various tunes (in *The Hymnal 1982*, The Episcopal Church)

Shepherd of Souls, Refresh and Bless, words by James Montgomery (1825), music "St. Agnes" by John B. Dykes (1866)

This Is the Hour of Banquet and of Song, words by Horatius Bonar (1855), various tunes (in *The Hymnal 1982*, The Episcopal Church)

While in Sweet Communion Feeding, words by Edward Denny (1796-1889), music by Edward J. Hopkins

Zion, Praise Thy Savior, Singing, words by St. Thomas Aquinas (1263), translated in *The Hymnal 1940*.

A rich collection of communion hymns is the *Chalice Hymnal* (St. Louis: Chalice Press, 1995), which serves the Disciples of Christ, who partake of the Lord's Supper each week. The hymnal contains 50 such hymns. For older communion hymns, a rich resource is *Christian Worship: A Hymnal* (Christian Board of Publication; St. Louis: The Bethany Press, 1941). *The Hymnal 1982* (The Episcopal Church; Church Hymnal Corporation, 1985) is also a rich collection of mainly older songs, some translated from ancient hymns.

Appendix 4: Introduction to Textual Criticism

If you've ever studied the New Testament in a group where some use the King James Version and others use newer translations such as the New International Version or the New American Standard Bible, you've probably observed on occasion that the KJV includes phrases that aren't found in newer

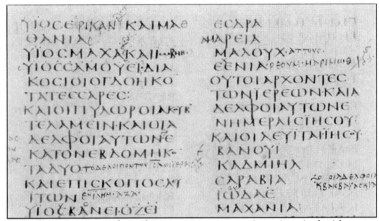

Codex Sianaticus is an Alexandrian text-type manuscript written in the 4th century in uncial letters on parchment. Preserved at the Monastery of St. Catherine near Mt. Sinai, now most is at the British Museum.

translations. I want try to explain why in as simple a way as possible, even though this is a very complex subject.

But first, I realize that when I talk about Textual Criticism some will confuse it with "Higher Criticism" that sometimes seemed like a synonym for modern unbelief. That's completely different. Textual Criticism is the fancy name for the discipline of determining as closely as possible which was the original text of a New Testament Gospel or Epistle as it came from the pen of its divinely inspired author or his secretary. Sometimes people choke on the word "criticism." It doesn't mean to criticize everything; it is a technical term that means "the scientific investigation of literary documents (as in the Bible) in regard to such matters as origin, text, composition, or history."[1]

Types of Copying Errors

We take Xerox copy machines for granted. But in ancient times manuscripts were laboriously – and lovingly – copied by hand, letter after letter, line after line, page after page. If you've ever copied something out of a book, not to mention someone's slightly illegible handwriting, you know that it's easy to make mistakes, even if you check for

---

[1] *Merriam Webster's Collegiate Dictionary* (Tenth Edition; Merriam-Webster, 1993), p. 275.

mistakes again and again. The same kind of minor errors affected copies of various Bible books, too.

- Incorrect divisions between words (spaces were often missing in early manu- scripts).
- Confusing one letter for another.
- Skipping from one word to another with a similar ending, omitting a whole group of words.
- Writing a word twice.
- Transposing letters or words.
- Mistakes in understanding a word pronounced by a reader.
- Hearing one word and then inadvertently writing down another with the same meaning.
- Correcting what were considered grammatical or linguistic errors.
- Eliminating apparent discrepancies.
- Harmonizing one gospel with another.

Most of the changes were minor and unintentional. Only rarely would copyists change something so it conformed better with a current doctrinal understanding. Consider how many miniscule errors might be present in a single hand-copied Greek manuscript of the Gospel of Luke. If you counted them all they might number in the hundreds, but have little effect and lie unnoticed.

Autographs and Manuscript Families

But copies of New Testament books weren't just copied a single time. There were copies of copies of copies of copies. Assuming that the original New Testament book or epistle (the "autograph") was without any grammatical or spelling error, each copy of the original would contain some minor errors.

Each copy of the copies would contain the errors of their parent manuscripts and then introduce their own. All told, we've found about 9,000 Greek manuscripts that contain all or part of the New Testament. If you were to conduct a minute study – and believe me, scholars have – you could construct "families" of copies based on certain characteristic errors that have been preserved and carried down from an early copy to the hundreds of copies that have been made from it.

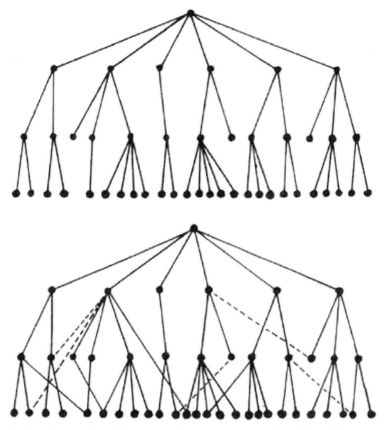

The first diagram shows how copies of manuscripts were derived from the original 'Autograph'. The second diagram shows greater complexity with some copies showing influences from other manuscript families. From J. H. Greenlee, *Introduction to New Testament Textual Criticism* (Eerdmans, 1964), p. 14.

External Evidence: The "Earliest" Manuscripts

Scholars have found four major manuscript "families": Alexandrian, Caesarean, Western, and Byzantine. Some of the most important manuscripts containing most or all of the New Testament are named by Latin or Greek letters. The papyrus manuscripts are given a letter P with a superscript, such as P^1 or P^{75}. Then you have early translations, such as into Latin, Ethiopic, Syrian, Armenian, etc. In addition there are quotations of many verses in the writings of the Early Church Fathers.

A careful study of characteristic errors in a manuscript may help a scholar place it as "early" (few errors, except the errors common to its family) or "later" (more errors, both the common family errors as well as others that had been introduced). If you want to get as close as possible to the New Testament as the inspired Apostles wrote it – and that's our goal – you look for evidence in the very earliest manuscripts. All other things being equal, a particular wording that is attested by several of the earliest manuscripts found in several families is more likely to be correct that the wording found only in an older manuscript all from the same family. Displaying the various manuscripts and families that line up for one wording or another is call examining the "external evidence." When you do this, it frequently becomes obvious which wording (or "reading") is the earliest.

Internal Evidence: Four Guidelines in Textual Criticism

But not always. In some cases, there is strong evidence for two or three different wordings. At that point scholars look for "internal evidence" to guide them to the wording most likely to be the original. Though they aren't set in stone, scholars have developed four principles that guide their thinking about any given wording variation.

1. **The shorter wording is often preferable**. It's generally easier to explain words being added on than words being deleted.
2. **The harder wording is often preferable**. We have a tendency to want to smooth out choppy grammar or "difficult" sayings, to soften them and make them a bit more understandable. Thus, the more "difficult" wording is more likely to be original than a smoother wording.
3. **The wording from which the other wordings in a variant could most easily develop is preferable**. Some of these are like puzzles. When you study them long enough, you can figure out how each of the different wordings could develop from one of the wordings, and if you can do that, you're likely to be correct.
4. **The wording which is most characteristic of the author is generally preferable**. Each of the New Testament authors has his own writing style. It just makes sense that when there's a question, the style most often used by a particular author is the earliest one.[2]

Though these principles are helpful, you can see that this is pretty subjective. The great majority of the time, using either external or internal evidence or both, you can be pretty sure of how the original "autograph" was worded. But in a few hundred cases,

[2] J. Harold Greenlee, *Introduction to New Testament Textual Criticism* (Eerdmans, 1964), pp. 114-115.

we just can't be as sure. Usually those cases will show up in newer translations as footnotes displaying an alternate wording.

In addition to technical commentaries, the most helpful book I've found, that discusses these decisions between one wording and another, is Bruce M. Metzger, *A Textual Commentary on the Greek New Testament* (United Bible Societies, 1971, 1995). As you might guess, you need to know some Greek to make much sense out of it. But if you do understand Greek, you'll find this book quite useful.

Does It Make Any Difference?

You may wonder if this textual criticism stuff makes any difference. The answer is "A little." Today we have an extremely good idea what the original "autograph" manuscripts of the New Testament Gospels and Epistles said – much better, for example than 400 years ago when the King James Version was translated, relying very heavily on just one manuscript family, the Byzantine family.

Here are examples of two passages that read differently in newer translations than in the KJV due to our better understanding of what was the original wording:

Mark 9:29

And he said unto them, This kind can come forth by nothing, but by prayer *and fasting*. (KJV)

He replied, "This kind can come out only by prayer." (NIV)

Metzger comments,

"In light of the increasing stress in the early church on the necessity of fasting it is understandable that ['and fasting'] is a gloss which found its way into most witnesses. Among the witnesses that resisted such an accretion are important representatives of the Alexandrian, the Western, and the Caesarean types of text."

The committee Metzger worked with scored this as an "A" probability, "A" meaning quite certain and "D" being uncertain.[3]

Luke 9:54-56

And when his disciples James and John saw this, they said, Lord, wilt thou that we command fire to come down from heaven, and consume them, *even as Elias did*? But he turned, and rebuked them, *and said, Ye know not what manner of spirit ye are of. For the Son of man is not come to destroy men's lives, but to save them.* And they went to another village. (KJV)

---

[3] Metzger, *Textual Commentary*, p. 101.

When the disciples James and John saw this, they asked, "Lord, do you want us to call fire down from heaven to destroy them?" But Jesus turned and rebuked them, and they went to another village. (NIV)

Metzger comments:

"The reading 'even as Elias did,' as well as the longer readings in verses 55 and 56, had fairly wide circulation in parts of the ancient church. The absence of the clauses, however, from such early witnesses as P45,75 Aleph B L Xi 1241 it[1] syr[s] cop[sa,bo] suggests that they are glosses derived from some extraneous source, written or oral."

Metzger's committee scores this as a "C" probability, somewhat uncertain.[4]

I could go on, but that gives you the idea.

Can We Believe the Bible?

After reading all this you might get the idea that you can't really believe the Bible. Not so. I've delved into these matters and believe even more strongly than before that the Bible we have today *can* be trusted, and is more reliable even than the Bibles that were available a couple of centuries ago. No major doctrine of Christianity is affected by *any* of the common wording variations. These involve minor points only. The thousands of Greek manuscripts that exist are strong evidence to the certainty and trustworthiness of our Bible.

[4] Metzger, pp. 148-149.

Appendix 5: Handouts for Classes and Groups

If you're working with a class or small group, feel free to duplicate the following handouts in this appendix at no additional charge. If you'd like to print 8-1/2" x 11" sheets, you can download the free Participant Guide handout sheets at:

www.jesuswalk.com/lords-supper/lords-supper-lesson-handouts.pdf

Discussion Questions

You'll find 4-5 questions for each lesson. Each question may include several sub-questions. These are designed to get group members engaged in discussion of the key points of the passage. If you're running short of time, feel free to skip questions or portions of questions.

1. My Body, My Blood – Literal or Figurative?
   Brief Glossary of the Lord's Supper
2. Remembering and Proclaiming Christ's Death (Luke 22:19b; 1 Cor. 11:23-26)
3. Being Sharers in the Sacrifice (1 Corinthians 10:16, 18)
4. My Body Given for You (Luke 22:19b)
5. My Blood Poured Out for Many (Matthew 26:28)
6. A New Covenant in My Blood (1 Corinthians 11:25)
7. The Cup of Blessing and the One Loaf (1 Corinthians 10:16-17)
8. Eating His Flesh, Drinking His Blood (John 6:53-57)
9. The Lord's Supper and the Great Banquet (Luke 22:16, 18; Matthew 26:29)
10. Preparing Ourselves for the Lord's Supper (1 Corinthians 11: 27-34)

1. My Body, My Blood – Literal or Figurative?

Lord's Supper: Meditations for Disciples

Bread	*has a relationship to*	Jesus' Body
Wine	*has a relationship to*	Jesus' Blood

The Words of Institution

Matthew 26	Mark 14	Luke 22	1 Cor 11
[26]While they were eating, Jesus took bread, gave thanks and **broke it**, and gave it to his disciples, saying, **"Take and eat; this is my body."**	[22]While they were eating, Jesus took bread, gave thanks and **broke it**, and gave it to his disciples, saying, **"Take it; this is my body."**	[19]And he took bread, gave thanks and **broke it**, and gave it to them, saying, **"This is my body given for you**; do this in remembrance of me."	[23b]The Lord Jesus, on the night he was betrayed, took bread, [24]and when he had given thanks, he **broke it** and said, **"This is my body, which is for you**; do this in remembrance of me."
[27]Then he took the cup, gave thanks and offered it to them, saying, "Drink from it, all of you. [28]**This is my blood of the covenant**, which is **poured out for many** for the **forgiveness of sins."**	[23]Then he took the cup, gave thanks and offered it to them, and they all drank from it. [24]**"This is my blood of the covenant**, which is poured out for many," he said to them.	[20]In the same way, after the supper he took the cup, saying, **"This cup is the new covenant in my blood**, which is **poured out for you."**	[25]In the same way, after supper he took the cup, saying, **"This cup is the new covenant in my blood**; do this, whenever you drink it, in remembrance of me."

Circle each of the important words in these passages, and connect the ones that are the same or similar to each other with lines. What do you learn by this exercise?

| Bread | has a **literal** relationship to | Jesus' Body |
| Bread | has a **figurative** relationship to | Jesus' Body |

How is Christ Present in Communion

1. **Transubstantiation** (change in substance), corporeal presence or Real Presence
2. **Sacramental Union** (sometimes called Consubstantiation, same substance), Luther
3. **Symbolic and Spiritual Presence**, Calvin

The Argument for a Literal Interpretation of the Words of Institution

1. Jesus' discourse in John 6:54-57 uses very _____ language, which can only refer to the Eucharist.
2. Nowhere in the Words of Institution is a hint that a _____ interpretation should be considered.
3. Paul's language, "Guilty of the body and blood of the Lord" (1 Corinthians 11:27) requires that Christ is c_____or b_____ present in the Lord's Supper.
4. The Church has taken the Words of Institution _____ rather than figuratively from the earliest times. (Argument from tradition.)

The Argument for a Figurative Interpretation of the Words of Institution

1. Jesus' words should be seen in the context of many _____.
2. Jesus held the bread in his _____ when he said "This is my body."
3. The phrase "this cup is a new covenant" (Luke 22:20) surely doesn't mean that the physical _____ is the new _____.
4. John 6:27-59 uses bold terms to explain a _____ feeding on Christ.
5. Paul's reference to "sinning against the body and blood of the Lord" in 1 Corinthians 11:17 does _____ require the Real Presence to explain it.
6. The Real Presence (rather than a spiritual presence) in the elements isn't taught in the _____ for at least 75 years and perhaps twice that.

Q1. How does your particular understanding of the bread and the wine (literal or figurative) help you grow closer to Christ when partaking of the Lord's Supper?

The Body and Blood of the Lord

"The body and blood of the Lord" (1 Corinthians 11:27; 10:16). How should we treat these elements?

Not "Mere Symbols"

Doctrine of the "Real Absence" of Christ in the sacrament. (Erickson, *Christian Theology*)

Q2. How can an extreme symbolic interpretation cause a person to have too little respect for the Lord's Supper and its elements? Where is the balance, do you think?

Actions on the Bread and Wine

The Real Presence controversy is based on interpreting a **verb of being** ("is"), though the original Aramaic that Jesus would have spoken wouldn't have contained such a verb. The real key to understanding Jesus' intent lies instead in observing the **action verbs** contained in the Words of Institution. Most of these are pretty straightforward words – no big mystery, no deep meanings.

Bread

"Given" (Luke), *didōmi*, here used with the meaning, "to dedicate oneself for some purpose or cause, give up, sacrifice."[10] Used with a similar meaning at 2 Corinthians 8:5; Matthew 20:28; Mark 10:45; 1 Timothy 2:6; Galatians 1:14; Titus 2:14

"Broken for" (KJV), *klaō*, " appears as a variant reading in 1 Corinthians 11:24b. We'll discuss this further in Chapter 4.

Wine

"Poured out" ("shed," KJV), *ekcheō*, "cause to be emitted in quantity, pour out." In the cultic sense, "pour out" (compare Leviticus 4:7), especially of Jesus' death, "blood shed for (the benefit of) many..."

"Forgiveness" ("remission" KJV), *aphesis*, is actually a noun, but it describes an action. It means, "the act of freeing from an obligation, guilt, or punishment, pardon, cancellation."

Q3. Which action words used to describe the elements of the Lord's Supper, teach us that we are to be thinking of Jesus' sacrifice of atonement, when we partake of the Lord's Supper?

Meaning intended for the Lord's Supper

1. Is symbolic of _____ and _____.

2. _____ us to Christ's sacrifice on the cross in some mystical way.

3. Is a powerful way of _____ Christ's death.

4. Is a way of renewing the _____.

5. Is a way to look forward to the fellowship of all the saints with Christ on the _____.

6. Keeps us focused on Christ's _____.

Q4. Which part of the meaning of the Lord's Supper is most valuable for you at this point in your spiritual journey when you partake of and meditate on the Lord's Supper?

Answers. Literal Interpretation: 1. literal, 2. figurative, 3. corporeal, bodily, 4. literally. Figurative Interpretation: 1. parables, 2. hand, 3. cup, covenant, 4. spiritual, 5. not, 6. early church. Meaning Intended: 1. nourishment, sustenance, 2. connects, 3. remembering, 4. Covenant, 5. Last Day, 6. death.

Brief Glossary of the Lord's Supper

Words for the Lord's Supper

Lord's Supper is used directly in 1 Corinthians 11:20 to describe this ceremony of remembrance. This word is common in most denominations. The term **Last Supper** refers to the historical event which took place the day before Jesus' crucifixion at which he instituted or began the practice of the Lord's Supper.

Communion, from Latin *communion-, communio*, "mutual participation," from *communis*. The Latin Vulgate translates the Greek word *koinōnia* in 1 Corinthians 10:16 this way. The King James Version (KJV) translates *koinōnia* as "communion" here also. This idea of mutual sharing has come into English as "communion," and emphasizes both the way that the Lord's Supper unites God's people and the communion we have with Christ at the Table. This word is very common among Protestant groups, such as Methodists, Presbyterians, Baptists, and others, and is often referred to as Holy Communion.

Eucharist, from Greek *eucharisteō*, "be thankful," comes from the account that Jesus "gave thanks" (Matthew 26:27, Mark 14:23, Luke 22:19, 1 Corinthians 11:24) before presenting to his followers the bread and the wine. This word is more common in liturgical churches such as Roman Catholic, Anglican, and Episcopal.

Mass is used by Roman Catholics, Anglo-Catholics, and some High Church Lutherans to refer to the service of the Lord's Supper. The word comes from Vulgar Latin *messa*, literally, "dismissal at the end of a religious service," and Late Latin, "to send." A related word **missal** is a book containing all that is said or sung at mass during the entire year.

Maundy Thursday refers to the day on which the Lord's Supper took place, which some churches celebrate with a Maundy Thursday service. Maundy comes from the Latin *mandatum*, "command" from which we get our English word "mandate." That night Jesus said, "A new command I give you: Love one another. As I have loved you, so you must love one another" (John 13:34).

Agape Feast or **Love Feast** is another term in Scripture for the Lord's Supper (Jude 12), used especially these days by the House Church movement. *Agapē* is the Greek word most often used to describe "selfless love." Generally an Agape Feast refers to a full meal that Christians have together, during which the bread and wine are eaten, such as was the practice in Corinth and the early church (1 Corinthians 11:20-22; Acts 2:46; Jude 12).

The Breaking of Bread (Acts 2:42, 46; 20:7) is another way the early church referred to the Lord's Supper.

Divine Liturgy is the term often used by the Byzantine tradition – Eastern Orthodox, Oriental Orthodox, and some Eastern-Rite Catholic churches. The word "liturgy" comes from Greek *leitourgia*, "public service." In English it refers to a rite or body of rites prescribed for public worship. **Holy Qurbana**, or **"Holy Sacrifice"** is the term used by the Chaldean and Syriac Christian Rites. **Badarak** is the term in the Armenian Church.

Host is a term sometimes used to describe a small, thin, round wafer used for communion, especially by those who believe in transubstantiation (see below). The word comes from Latin *hostia*, "victim, sacrificial animal," and is used in the Roman Catholic tradition and occasionally by Anglicans.

Chalice, from the Latin *calix*, "cup," is a goblet intended for drinking during a ceremony.

Cup is the term used in the New Testament to refer the drinking vessel (and often the wine contained within the vessel) used in the Lord's Supper (Matthew 26:27; Mark 14:23; Luke 22:20; 1 Corinthians 10:16, 21; 11:25-26).

Table of the Lord (1 Corinthians 10:21) is another way of referring to the Lord's Supper, emphasizing the host who invites people to a meal in his presence, fulfilled in heaven (Luke 22:30). In the Old Testament the term "Lord's table" referred to the priesthood's ministry of sacrifice and offering (Malachi 1:7, 12).

Sacraments vs. Ordinances

What should we call this action of partaking of the Lord's Supper? There are several terms used to describe this kind of religious act:

Sacrament (from Latin *sacrare*, "to consecrate"), is probably the most common term, defined in the dictionary as, "a Christian rite (as baptism or the Eucharist) that is believed to have been ordained by Christ and that is held to be a means of divine grace or to be a sign or symbol of a spiritual reality." Catholics recognize seven sacraments (Eucharist, baptism, ordination, penance, confession, marriage, and last rites). Most Protestants recognize two sacraments (the Lord's Supper and baptism).

Ordinance (from Latin *ordinare*, "to set in order, appoint"), "a prescribed usage, practice, or ceremony." Sometimes this word is used instead of sacrament by those who want to deemphasize what they would consider "magical" ideas that have been associated with the term "sacrament." They use ordinance to emphasize Christ's direct command and usually restrict the term "ordinance" to the Lord's Supper or baptism.

Rite and Ritual (from Latin *rites*, "number") is a more general term meaning in this context, "a prescribed form or manner governing the words or actions for a ceremony; the ceremonial practices of a church or group of churches." The Lord's Supper can properly be referred to as an ordinance, a sacrament, or a rite, depending upon your tradition. Some Christians use the term "ritual" with a bit of contempt, but if you observe them, they come to use the same prescribed words again and again, such as wedding vows or words at the Lord's Table.

Rites and rituals are not wrong. They are human ways in which we reverently set apart certain events as special, as sacred. Being critical of other Christians' rites and traditions shows our own narrowness, parochialism, and critical spirit more than the supposed purity of our doctrine or the superiority of our freedom in Christ.

The Presence of Christ in the Sacrament

Transubstantiation. (trans- = "change") The miraculous change by which according to Roman Catholic and Eastern Orthodox dogma the Eucharistic elements at their consecration become the body and blood of Christ while keeping only the appearances of bread and wine.

Sacramental Union (sometimes called Consubstantiation, con- = "same"). The actual substantial presence and combination of the body and blood of Christ with the Eucharistic bread and wine according to a teaching associated with Martin Luther.

Real Presence. Catholics believe in the *corporeal presence* or *Real Presence* of Christ in the sacrament, that the bread becomes Christ's body, and that when they partake they are taking in Christ's actual body.

Celebrate, Perform, Partake

While we're at it, let's clarify the *verbs* that describe the Lord's Supper in our day. Different traditions use different verbs. I share this so you'll be able to understand when other Christians relate the Lord's Supper in their own tradition and not be offended by their terminology.

Celebrate, in this context, means "to perform (a sacrament or solemn ceremony) publicly and with appropriate rites," such as in "celebrate the mass." Some Protestants use "celebrate" to mean to praise God with joy and exuberance. Don't confuse this connotation with "celebrate" in connection with the Lord's Supper. That's really a different and separate use of the word. The person who officiates at the Lord's Supper is technically referred to as the "celebrant."

Perform, in this context, means "to do in a formal manner or according to a prescribed ritual."

Partake of, as in the phrase, "partake of the Lord's Supper," means to eat and drink the communion elements.

Enact, to act out. In a sense we act out the Last Supper, breaking the bread, offering prayers and blessings, and distributing the elements to those present.

Most English definitions and etymologies are from *Merriam-Webster's 11th Collegiate Dictionary* (2003).

2. Remembering and Proclaiming Christ's Death (Luke 22:19b; 1 Cor. 11:23-26)

Lord's Supper: Meditations for Disciples

"This is my body given for you; **do this in remembrance of me.**" (Luke 22:19b)

"[23]For I received from the Lord what I also passed on to you: The Lord Jesus, on the night he was betrayed, 'took bread, [24]and when he had given thanks, he broke it and said, 'This is my body, which is for you; **do this in remembrance of me.**' [25]In the same way, after supper he took the cup, saying, 'This cup is the new covenant in my blood; **do this, whenever you drink it, in remembrance of me.**' [26]For whenever you eat this bread and drink this cup, you **proclaim** the Lord's death until he comes." (1 Corinthians 11:23-26)

The Command to "Do This" Continually (Luke 22:19b)

Present tense can carry the idea of continuous action in the present. The present imperative has a "durative force." Present Imperative: "Do this and keep on doing it."

Q1. When repeated often, doesn't the Lord's Supper run the risk of becoming mundane and lose its meaning? Why did Jesus command its repetition?

Passover as a Memorial Feast or Seder

Read: Exodus 12:14-15, 24-27

At a contemporary Seder the table is set with:

1. **Unleavened bread or Matzoh** to remind them that there wasn't time for bread to rise; they left Egypt in a hurry.
2. **Haroseth** represents the mortar used to build buildings for Pharaoh.
3. **Bitter herbs** are reminiscent of the bitter affliction of slavery.
4. **Parsley dipped in salt water** reminds them of the tears of the Jewish slaves.
5. **Roasted egg** is a symbol of Spring.
6. **Lamb's meat** was part of the meal (before sacrifices were ended in 70 AD). These days a **shank bone** reminds participants of the Passover lamb.
7. **Four cups of wine**, each with a different meaning are part of the meal – representing freedom, deliverance, redemption, and release.
8. **A fifth cup** of wine in the contemporary Jewish Seder, the Cup of Elijah, looks forward to the coming of the Messiah.

During the meal the youngest member of the family is coached to ask and answer questions, such as, **"Why is this day different from all other days?"** This prompts a retelling of the story of how God delivered the people of Israel from Egypt during the Exodus.

Q2. What was the purpose of the Passover meal for future generations? Why was it to be repeated? What was to be remembered? What would have happened if the Jews had stopped remembering the Exodus?

In Remembrance of Me

"In" *eis*, motion into a thing or towards a goal, used to denote a purpose, "in order to," or for the purpose of remembrance.

"Remembrance," *anamnēsis*, means "remembrance, reminder, recollection." This isn't just a passive memory, but an active "reliving of vanished impressions by a definite act of will.".

Q3. Why is our remembrance of Christ's death so important? What happens to Christianity if we neglect remembering in this way? What happens to us personally when we forget Christ's death?

Proclaiming the Lord's Death (1 Corinthians 11:26)

"Proclaim" (NIV, NRSV) or "shew" (KJV) is *katangellō*, "to make known in public, with implication of broad dissemination." The word is frequently used in literature of public decrees. The word is often used in the Acts and Paul for preaching the message of Jesus, for declaring the Christian gospel.

Read: 1 Corinthians 2:1-2

Q4. (1 Corinthians 11:26) In what way is the Lord's Supper a proclamation? To whom is the proclamation made? Why is this important? What happens to the church when its proclamation shifts to a different central theme?

3. Being Sharers in the Sacrifice (1 Corinthians 10:16, 18)

Lord's Supper: Meditations for Disciples

Using 1 Corinthians 10:16-22 below or in your own Bible circle all the following words:

- NIV – participation/participation/participants/have a part in
- KJV – communion/partakers of
- NRSV/NASB – sharing/partners in/sharers in

Each of these words renders the Greek word *koinōnia*

> "[14]Therefore, my dear friends, flee from idolatry. [15]I speak to sensible people; judge for yourselves what I say. [16]Is not the cup of thanksgiving for which we give thanks a participation in the blood of Christ? And is not the bread that we break a participation in the body of Christ? [17]Because there is one loaf, we, who are many, are one body, for we all partake of the one loaf.

> "[18]Consider the people of Israel: Do not those who eat the sacrifices participate in the altar? [19]Do I mean then that a sacrifice offered to an idol is anything, or that an idol is anything? [20]No, but the sacrifices of pagans are offered to demons, not to God, and I do not want you to be participants with demons. [21]You cannot drink the cup of the Lord and the cup of demons too; you cannot have a part in both the Lord's table and the table of demons. [22]Are we trying to arouse the Lord's jealousy? Are we stronger than he?" (1 Corinthians 10:16-22, NIV)

Q1. Why was Paul exhorting the Corinthians about the cup of the Lord and the cup of demons? What was going on in the church? What was the danger to the believers?

Participation, Communion, Koinōnia (1 Corinthians 10:16)

Koinōnia, "participation" (NIV) also translated as "communion" (KJV) or "sharing" (NRSV). It means sharing something in common with others. The root *koinē* means common in contrast to private or sacred – common ground, common pastureland, communal property, a couple's community property. When it refers to people it means "participants, fellows." The idea is that which is shared in common with others.

Q2. What does *koinōnia* mean? What does it mean to "participate" or "share" in the blood of Christ?

Eating a Portion of the Sacrifice for Sin

Read Leviticus 6:24-26 and 10:12-15.

Sharers in the Altar (1 Corinthians 10:18)

Q3. In what way did the priests participate in the altar by eating of the Old Testament sacrifices? How does Paul connect this observation with our participation with Christ's sacrifice?

Sharers in the Cross

Communion

Q4. What are the implications for you personally, when you realize that in the Lord's Supper you are becoming a sharer in the sacrifice of the cross? How does that affect you? How does it change your understanding of the Lord's Supper?

4. My Body Given for You (Luke 22:19b)

The Lord's Supper: Meditations for Disciples

Luke 22:19b This is my body **given for you.** Do this in remembrance of me.

1 Corinthians 11:24b This is my body which is **for you.** Do this in remembrance of me.

My Body which Is Broken for You (1 Corinthians 11:24b, KJV)

Psalm 34:20. The bread in the sacrament is broken, but that is not the center of our remembrance. It is not the *breaking* of Jesus' body but the *giving* of it that we are to focus on.

Jesus' Body Given for You (Luke 22:19b)

"Given," *didōmi*, used in Luke 22:19b, "to dedicate oneself for some purpose or cause, give up, sacrifice."

Preposition *hyper*, "in behalf of"

Ideas of: (1) sacrifice, (2) giving oneself, (3) voluntary giving

1. Jesus' Body as a Sacrifice

1 Peter 2:24 with Isaiah 53:5-6

Q1. (1 Peter 2:24) Why do you think the Apostle Peter emphasized Jesus' physical body, when he talks about sin-bearing?

 Also Romans 7:4; Hebrews 10:10, 5-7 (*soma*, "body")

1 Peter 3:18; 4:1; Hebrews 10:19-20; 1 John 4:2-3 (*sarx*, "flesh")

Q2. (1 John 4:2-3) Why does Christianity insist on a physical birth, physical suffering, and a resurrection of the physical body? How would our faith be different if Christ hadn't fully entered the human condition?

2. Jesus Gave Himself to Rescue and Ransom Us

Verb *didōmi*, "give," with the preposition *hyper*, "in behalf of."   1 Timothy 2:5-6; Galatians 1:3-4; Titus 2:13-14; Matthew 20:28 = Mark 10:45; Ephesians 5:2; also 1 Peter 3:18

Q3. Look at the verses above which include both the word "give" and a preposition that means "in behalf of." According to these verses, what was the purpose of Jesus giving himself in sacrifice?

3. He Voluntarily Laid Down His Life to Defend Us

Luke 22:42-44; John 18:11; also John 10:11, 14-15, 17; John 15:13

Q4. How does Jesus' voluntarily laying down his life for you encourage you? How does it speak to your value and worth as a person? What does it inspire you to do?

5. My Blood Poured Out for Many (Matthew 26:28)

Lord's Supper: Meditations for Disciples

> "This is my blood ... which is poured out for many for the forgiveness of sins." (Matthew 26:28)

Blood Reserved for Atonement

Leviticus 17:10-11

Blood Sacrifices in the Old Testament

Hebrews 9:22

Leviticus 4:27-35; Exodus 29:38; Yom Kippur, Leviticus 16; Psalm 51:16-17

Q1. How were Old Testament sacrifices a way of God showing grace and mercy to his people?

Sacrificing the Paschal Lamb

Exodus 12:7, 12-13; 1 Corinthians 5:7

Poured Out

"Poured out" ("shed," KJV), *ekcheō*, "cause to be emitted in quantity, pour out." The expression "shed blood" is used of the violent slaying of Old and New Testament martyrs (Matthew 23:35; Romans 3:15 = Isaiah 59:7; Acts 22:20; Revelation 16:6).

Q2. Why did Jesus refer to the violent nature of his death in the Words of Institution? What did this probably mean to the disciples at the time? What did it probably mean to them later?

For Many

> Matthew 26:28; Mark 10:45 = Matthew 20:28; Isaiah 53:11-12

Q3. Why did Jesus purposely point his disciples to the phrasing found in Isaiah 53? How does this chapter help explain the meaning of Jesus' death?

Christ's Blood in the New Testament

- Redemption: 1 Peter 1:18-19; Ephesians 1:7; Hebrews 9:12
- Purchase (a concept closely related to redemption): Revelation 5:9; Acts 20:28
- Forgiveness and Atonement: Romans 3:25; 5:9
- Sanctification, Cleansing, and Purification from Sin: Hebrews 9:14; 1 John 1:7; 1

Peter 1:2; Hebrews 13:12

- Freedom and Victory over Sin and Satan: Revelation 1:5; 12:11
- Reconciliation to and Peace with God: Ephesians 2:13; Colossians 1:19-20; Hebrews 10:19-20; 13:20-21

Depictions of the Blood of Christ

Songs about the Blood of Jesus

- "There Is a Fountain Filled with Blood, Drawn from Emmanuel's Veins," words by William Cowper (1772), music: 19th century American camp meeting tune.
- "There Is Power in the Blood," words and music by Lewis E. Jones (1899).
- "What Can Wash Away My Sin? Nothing but the Blood of Jesus," words and music by Robert Lowry (1876).
- "Oh, the Blood of Jesus, It Washes White as Snow" (unknown author)
- "Are You Washed in the Blood?" words and music by Elisha A. Hoffman (1878).
- "The Blood Will Never Lose Its Power," by Andraé Crouch (©1966 by Manna Music, Inc.)

Poured Out for the Forgiveness of Sin

"Forgiveness" ("remission" KJV), *aphesis*, means, "the act of freeing from an obligation, guilt, or punishment; pardon, cancellation."[6]

Isaiah 43:25; Jeremiah 31:34; Psalm 103:12; Micah 7:19

Q4. What do the Words of Institution say to us about forgiveness? Why is it important for us to repent of known sin before taking the Lord's Supper?

6. A New Covenant in My Blood (1 Corinthians 11:25)

Lord's Supper: Meditations for Disciples

Covenants in the Old Testament

Hebrew word *berît*, and the Greek noun *diathēkē*. A covenant is "a solemn commitment guaranteeing promises or obligations undertaken by one or both covenanting parties." Between nations a covenant is a treaty, an alliance. Between individuals it is a pledge or agreement. Between a king and his subjects it is a constitution. Between God and man it is a relationship with promises of blessing for keeping the covenant and curses for breaking it. Covenants were often ratified by signs, a solemn oath, and a meal. Sacrifice was often part of the process of ratifying a covenant, too, hence the phrase "to cut a covenant" (Genesis 15:9-10, 17; Jeremiah 34:18).

God's covenant with _____ (Genesis 6:8; 9:9-17),

God's covenant with _____ and his descendents (Genesis 15:18; 17:2-21),

God's covenant with _____ and the people of Israel at Mt. Sinai (Exodus 19:5; 24:7-8; 31:16; 34:10, 27; etc.).

Provisions of the Old Covenant

God's Obligations	Israel's Obligations
• God will be with Israel and lead them on their journey.	• Exclusive love for and allegiance to God, no other gods.
• God protect his people.	• Obedience to God's commandments.
• God will provide for and bless his people.	

Exodus 24:3-11

Q1. (Exodus 24:3-11) How was the covenant with Israel ratified? What promise did the people make twice in this passage? What was sacrificed? What was sprinkled? What was eaten?

God's Promise of a New Covenant

Jeremiah 31:31-34; Hebrews 8:6-13; 10:16-17.

Provisions of the New Covenant

Acts 2:38-39; Romans 8:9-11; 1 John 1:7, 9

Q2. (Jeremiah 31:31-34) How does the promised New Covenant differ from the Old Covenant? What are the promises God makes in the New Covenant? What are *our* responsibilities under the New Covenant?

Confirmation of the Covenant at a Meal

70 Elders (Exodus 24:11), Isaac and Abimelech (Genesis 26:30), Laban and Jacob (Genesis 31:46, 53-54); and Moses, the Israelites, and Jethro (Exodus 18:12).

The Lord's Supper as Confirming the Covenant

The Last Supper was a kind of covenant meal where Jesus introduces the New Covenant (Matthew 26:27-28).

1 Corinthians 11:25 extends the meal into the future.

Q3. What is the significance of the 12 Apostles drinking the Cup of the Covenant? To whom would they correspond under the ratification of the Old Covenant? (Hint: Exodus 24:11.) What is the significance of *us* drinking the Cup of the Covenant?

The Meal as Giving and Receiving Hospitality

Genesis 18:1-8; 19:1-8; John 13:18, quoting Psalm 41:9; Obadiah 1:7; Psalm 23:5; Revelation 3:20

Q4. Why is the Lord's Table such a time of intimate fellowship with Jesus? In your experience with having meals with friends, what makes the difference between a casual, forgettable meal, and one which is rich with memories? How can this insight make your experience of the Lord's Table more meaningful?

Invitation to the Covenant

Revelation 21:6; 22:17; Isaiah 55:1-3; Matthew 26:28; Hebrews 13:20-21

Answers: Noah, Abraham, Moses.

7. The Cup of Blessing and the One Loaf (1 Corinthians 10:16-17)

Lord's Supper: Meditations for Disciples

The Cup of Blessing

Jewish meals where blessings and thanksgivings were offered to God at the beginning and end of the meal, such as: "Blessed are You, O Lord our God, who have created the fruit of the vine." The cup of blessing was a Jewish technical term for the cup of wine, for which a blessing, i.e. thanksgiving, was given to God.

Q1. (1 Corinthians 10:16). What does the "cup of blessing" teach us about our focus at the Lord's Supper? Who is to be blessed when the "cup of blessing" is lifted heavenward?

We Partake of the One Loaf (1 Corinthians 10:17)

"Bread" (KJV, NRSV, NASB) or "loaf" (NIV) is the common word *artos*, "a baked product produced from a cereal grain, bread," also, "loaf of bread."

The One Loaf as a Symbol of Unity

> "Because there is one loaf, we, who are many, are one body, for we all partake of the one loaf." (1 Corinthians 10:17)

Many things divided the Corinthians:

1. _____ to leaders. (1 Corinthians 1:10-13)
2. _____ issues. (5:1-13; 6:9-20)
3. _____syncretism (or mixing Christianity with idolatry) (8:1-13; 10:6-33)
4. Disputes between _____. (6:1-8)
5. _____Distinctions. (11:17-22)
6. Spiritual _____ (Chapters 12 and 14)
7. Doctrinal _____ (15:12ff)

It's Me, O Lord

Q2. Read Mark 11:25 and Matthew 5:23-24. How do these relate to Paul's teaching on the One Loaf (1 Corinthians 10:17)? What must we personally do to achieve unity to prepare ourselves to partake of the Lord's Supper righteously?

The Scandal of Christian Divisions

Q3. In what ways do the divisions in Corinth sound familiar in our own congregations? Don't pick on another congregation; how about your own? How serious was the need for unity? Can bickering congregations partake of the Lord's Supper without sin?

Q4. (1 Corinthians 10:17) How does Paul's teaching on the One Loaf affect our relationships and love for those of other Christian denominations and traditions? How does blanket judgmentalism towards the faith of other Christian groups sometimes seem to excuse us from Jesus' command to love one another?

Answers. Dividers: 1. allegiance, 2. moral, 3. religious, 4. members, 5. class, 6. gifts, 7. disputes.

8. Eating His Flesh, Drinking His Blood (John 6:53-57)

Lord's Supper: Meditations for Disciples

Context, Themes, and Parables

Context:

Outline:

1. Jesus, the True Manna (6:27-34)
2. Jesus, the Bread of Life (6:35-51)
3. Partaking of the Son of Man (6:52-59)
4. Reactions to Jesus' Teaching (6:60-71)

Themes:

1. Believing on and continuing to trust in Jesus will bring a person to eternal life and ultimate resurrection in the Last Day (6:39-40, 47, 57, 63, etc.).
2. But this is entirely from God, since no one can come to Jesus unless the Father draws him, and Jesus will not lose any of them (6:44-46, 65).

Metaphors or Parables:

1. **Manna**, "bread from heaven" (6:31-34, 38, 41-42, 49-50, 58)
2. **Bread of Life**, that is, bread that brings about eternal life (6:35-42, 51, 58)
3. **Flesh and blood** as "food" (6:51b-56)

1. Jesus, the True Manna (6:27-34)

2. Jesus, the Bread of Life (6:35-51)

"I AM" passages in John (6:35; 8:12; 10:9; 10:11; 11:25; 14:6; 15:1; see Exodus 3:14).

| verse 47 | He who believes | has eternal life |
| verse 51a | If anyone eats of this (living) bread | he will live forever |

Q1. (John 6:35-51) What does the metaphor of "eating the Bread of Life" mean in practical terms? To extend the same metaphor, what do you think might be the difference between nibbling and actually making a meal of it?

Flesh Given for the Life of the World (6:51b)

"flesh"   *sarx*   "body, physical body."

"give, given"   *didōmi*   "to dedicate oneself for some purpose or cause, give up, sacrifice."

"for"   *hyper*   "in behalf of, for the sake of someone or something."

| Luke 22:19b | And he took **bread**, gave thanks and broke it, and gave it to them, saying, This is | **my body** (*sōma*) | given | for | you... |
| John 6:51b | This **bread** is | **my flesh** (*sarx*) | which I will give | for | the life of the world. |

Q2. (John 6:51b) What is Jesus referring to when he says, "This bread is my flesh, which I will give for the life of the world"? What similarities do you see with Jesus' teaching at the Last Supper in Luke 22:19b?

3. Partaking of the Son of Man (6:52-59)

Arguments for Taking the Passage Literally of the Eucharist

Pohle: "Nothing hinders our interpreting the first part (6:26-48) metaphorically and understanding by 'bread of heaven' Christ Himself as the object of faith, to be received in a figurative sense as a spiritual food by the mouth of faith. Such a figurative explanation of the second part of the discourse (6:52-72), however, is not only unusual but absolutely impossible."

We are not required to go as far back as the Old Testament for the metaphor, just a few verses back where he speaks of eating the Bread of Life (6:50-51a). This is a continuation and intensification of that same metaphor. Jesus sums it up in verse 58 with a reference back to his previous words about the Bread of Life:

"This is the bread that came down from heaven. Your forefathers ate manna and died, but he who feeds on this bread will live forever." (6:58)

What Does Jesus Mean about Eating His Flesh, Drinking His Blood?

Ref	Consequence	Similar sayings elsewhere
6:53	Having life in oneself	The consequence of believing is to have life in his name, according to John 20:31. In 1 John 5:10-12, having life is associated with believing in the Son of God.
6:54a	Has eternal life	Eternal life is the consequence of believing in John 6:40a, as well as in John 3:15-16; 3:36; 5:24; 1 Timothy 1:16; 1 John 5:13; etc.
6:54b	Resurrection on the last day	Resurrection on the last day is the consequence of believing according to John 6:40b. Jesus also connects believing in him with resurrection and eternal life in the raising of Lazarus (John 11:25-26)
6:56	Remains or abides in Jesus	This is also a consequence of believing Jesus' words according to John 15:7. His word remaining or abiding in us is connected with eternal life (1 John 2:23-25), being true disciples (John 8:31-32), and bearing fruit (John 15:5).
6:57	Live because of me	The consequence of believing in the "I am the resurrection and the life" passage, John 11:25-26
6:58	Live forever	"Live forever" is the consequence of eating of the "living bread" in John 6:51b above. It is another way of saying one "has eternal life" (see 6:54a above). In John 11:26 Jesus connects believing in him with never dying.

4. Reactions to the Teaching (6:60-71)

Q3. (John 6:53-71) If to eat Jesus' flesh and drink his blood is a strong expression for "to believe," why does Jesus emphasize this so strongly? What was the difference between the Twelve and the crowd of "disciples" that turned away from Jesus? What is the mark of true disciples according to John 8:31-32?

The Spirit Gives Life, the Flesh Counts for Nothing (6:63)

What does "flesh" (*sarx*) refer to?

1. Eating my flesh = believing in Jesus. **The Spirit give life, believing in me counts for nothing.**

2. Eating my flesh = partaking of the Eucharist. **The Spirit gives life, eating the sacramental flesh counts for nothing.**

3. Flesh = the natural principle in man which cannot give eternal life. **The Spirit gives life; what man can understand and achieve on his own counts for nothing. The words I have spoken to you – spiritually discerned and believed – bring spiritual life, eternal life.**

The Bread of Life Passage and the Lord's Supper

Q4. How does "eating the Bread of Life" (to use Jesus' metaphor in John 6) nourish our faith? How does partaking of the Lord's Supper build and nourish our faith? What does the main point of the Bread of Life discourse (John 6:25-69) have in common with "Do this in remembrance of me," in Jesus' Words of Institution (1 Corinthians 11:23-26)?

9. The Lord's Supper and the Great Banquet (Luke 22:16, 18; Matthew 26:29)

Jewish Expectation of the Great Feast

Isaiah 25:6-8; Revelation 19:6-9; 21:4; Luke 14:15

> Yahweh will **recline at table**, the patriarchs and the righteous at His feet, and "They will recline at table and eat in Gan Eden," rabbinical commentary on Exodus.

> "At the last coming he will lead out Adam and the patriarchs and bring them (into the paradise of Eden) that they may rejoice, as when a man invites his friends to eat with him, and they come and speak with one another before the palace, joyously awaiting his **feast**, the enjoyment of good things, of immeasurable wealth and joy and happiness in light and everlasting life," pseudepigraphical Book of Enoch

> "Rise and stand, and see at the **feast** of the Lord the number of those who have been sealed," Old Testament Apocrypha.

> "The **feast** of our God, which He will prepare for the righteous, has no end," Midrash on Esther.

Jesus' Teaching on the Great Banquet

It was in this context that Jesus taught. He often alluded to the Great Feast in the Kingdom of God, both in parables and in direct comments. For example:

- Parable of the Great Banquet. Luke 14:18-24; Matthew 22:2-14
- Reward for the Apostles. Luke 22:29-30
- Teachings on Inclusion and Exclusion. ;Luke 13:29-30 || Matthew 8:11
- Parable of the Delayed Householder. Luke 12:37
- Parable of the Ten Virgins. Matthew 25:10
- Parable of the Rich Man and Lazarus. Luke 16:22
- Gathering the Elect. Mark 13:27 || Matthew 24:31

Q1. Why are so many of Jesus' teachings oriented toward the future? What kinds of associations come to mind as you think of the Great Banquet?

The Marriage Supper of the Lamb

Revelation 2:7; 19:6-9

The Lord's Supper Looks Forward to the Great Banquet

Matthew 26:29 || Mark 14:25; Luke 22:16.

"Fulfillment" is the verb *plēroō*, "to make full." – "1. to bring to a designed end, fulfill" a prophecy, a promise, etc., or "2. to bring to completion an activity in which one has been involved from its beginning, complete, finish."

Q2. (Luke 22:16) In what sense does the Lord's Supper find its "fulfillment" in the Great Banquet at the end of the age? What should this do to our thoughts at the Lord's Table?

The Promise of Future Fellowship

Hebrews 10:25

The Lord's Supper as a Promise of the Future

Q3. In what sense does the Lord's Supper point to the past? How does it point to the present? How does it point to the future?

We Shall See His Face

> "O I want to see Him, look upon His face,
> There to sing forever of His saving grace;
> On the streets of glory let me lift my voice,
> Cares all past, home at last, ever to rejoice."

John 1:18; 1 John 4:12; Revelation 22:4-5

Q4. (Revelation 22:4) When you meditate on "seeing his face," what thoughts come to mind? Why should the Lord's Supper stimulate these thoughts every time we partake of it?

10. Preparing Ourselves for the Lord's Supper (1 Corinthians 11: 27-34)

Lord's Supper: Meditations for Disciples

Divisions between the Rich and Poor in Corinth (11:17-22)

1 Corinthians 12:12-13

Not Discerning the Body (11:29)

"Discerning" (KJV, NRSV) or "recognizing" (NIV, NJB) is *dokimazō*, "to make a critical examination of something to determine genuineness, put to the test, examine," often used of assaying the genuineness of metal.... to discern, distinguish as distinct and different."

Two possible interpretations of the word "body" in verse 29:

1. "Body" refers to the Eucharistic elements.
2. "Body" refers to the church, the "Body of Christ (see 1 Corinthians 10:17)

Greek *anaxiōs* means "in an unworthy/careless manner." (Philippians 1:27; 1 Thessalonians 2:12; Colossians 1:10; Ephesians 4:1; 3 John 6).

Sinning against the Body and Blood of the Lord (1 Corinthians 11:27)

1 Corinthians 8:12; Matthew 25:31-46

Q1. (11:29) Why does "not discerning the body" at the Lord's Supper constitute such a grave sin? Aren't there worse things a church could have done?

Incurring Judgment and Discipline (1 Corinthians 11:29-32)

Two words are used to describe this punishment:

"Judgment" (NIV, NRSV, NKJV) or "damnation" (KJV) in verse 29 is *krima*, "legal decision rendered by a judge, judicial verdict."

"Disciplined" (NIV, NRSV) or "chastened" (KJV) in verse 32 is *paideuō*, "to assist in the development of a person's ability to make appropriate choices, practice discipline," here, to discipline with punishment, especially the kind of punishment a parent might give to a child to help mold his or her character.

Hebrews 12:5-7; 1 Corinthians 11:30

Q2. (1 Corinthians 11:29-32) Why has God brought judgment to the offending parties at Corinth? Isn't sickness and death rather harsh? How does God's discipline actually work for our good in the light of Hebrews 12:5-7?

Self-Examination (1 Corinthians 11:28, 31)

Two words to describe this:

1. **"Examine" yourself** (verse 28), *dokimazō*, "to make a critical examination of something to determine genuineness, put to the test, examine"
2. **"Judge" yourself** (vs. 31), *diakrinō*, used twice in this passage to mean, "to evaluate by paying careful attention to, evaluate, judge."

2 Corinthians 13:5; Galatians 6:4-5

Q3. (1 Corinthians 11:28, 31) Introspection by a neurotic person can foster guilt and self-loathing. Where is the balance? How can we conduct self-examination and self-judgment so that it has a healthy rather than an unhealthy result in us?

Confession and Repentance

Matthew 5:23-24; Mark 11:25; 1 John 1:9; Psalm 32:5; 51:2-5; 2 Corinthians 6:1

Q4. How do confession and repentance fit with self-examination? What is the result of self-examination without confession and repentance? How do confession and repentance serve to bring spiritual health and character change?

How to Prepare for Communion

1. Take some time _____ the communion service.
2. _____ yourself to see if you are in sin,
3. _____ any sins,
4. _____ of these sins
5. _____ God's forgiveness. (1 John 1:9)

Answer: 1. time, 2. examine, 3. confess, 4. repent, 5. accept.

CPSIA information can be obtained at www.ICGtesting.com
Printed in the USA
BVOW061834260812

298853BV00003B/70/P